The Gun Book *for* Parents

Silvio Calabi, Steve Helsley & Roger Sanger

SHOOTING
SPORTSMAN
BOOKS

ISBN 978-1-60893-201-6

Library of Congress Cataloging-in-Publication Data available upon request

Printed in the USA

5 4 3 2 1

 Books

Distributed to the trade by National Book Network

Designed by Rich Eastman

This book is dedicated to our parents, who aided and abetted our fledgling efforts as shooters—although they weren't shooters themselves—and to the knowledgeable gun men who became our mentors. Thank you all.

CONTENTS

What This Book Is About

The Shooting Sports in a Post-Modern World

*T*he Gun Book for Parents is a companion volume to *The Gun Book for Boys*, by the same authors and from the same publisher. The boys' book is for bright, inquisitive youngsters who want to know "all about guns," and it includes what he (or she) must know in order to have fun shooting safely.

This book is a straightforward treatment of common parental concerns about guns and shooting, from safety and legality to costs and benefits. (Shooting can be an engrossing family activity, and it offers a surprising range of career choices.) It is meant to reduce a parent's anxiety by an-

pen all by itself, sometimes to the puzzlement (if not the dismay) of non-shooting parents. *Where did this come from?* It seems natural, somehow. Guns can be fascinating historical artifacts and outstanding examples of craftsmanship, design and engineering. And shooting is not only enjoyable; like any sport, it emphasizes skill and personal achievement through discipline. Hunting aside, there are dozens of well-established, safe and regulated forms of shooting that can take a youngster all the way to the Olympic Games.

However, shooting requires a degree of responsibility that is sometimes more than ado-

Egad! Is this thing legal? This is a Russian military *Snayperskaya Vintovka Dragunova,* the Dragunov sniper rifle, and it is perfectly legal in the US—in some states. Fear of guns is rooted in ignorance. This book is intended to replace fear and ignorance with knowledge. A youngster who absorbs *The Gun Book for Boys* will have a grasp of shooting fundamentals that few adults do; and an involved parent who backs up that youngster with what's in this book will understand what's going on.

swering questions such as how to buy a gun and store it safely, where to shoot, and how to assess a child's behavior with guns.

We're not here to convince you or your kids to take up shooting; often that seems to hap-

lescents can reliably manage. This book, then, is for you, the parent, and it presents the adult side: what you need to know in order to keep your young shooters out of trouble and to support them in their interests.

We, the authors, grew up in the 1950s and '60s and learned to shoot and handle guns the time-honored, old-fashioned way: haphazardly and from an odd variety of sources—at least half of which, or whom, were wrong at least half the time. In other words, the same way many of us learned about sex, money and alcohol. Somehow 99.999 percent of us survived this trial-and-error process, but we don't recommend it.

As well, that was a very different time in America. Many large high schools had shooting ranges. The sight of a 14-year-old boy with a .22 rifle across the handlebars of his bicycle didn't prompt hysterical reactions. No one called the police.

Times have changed. Nearly three-quarters of Americans live in urban areas now, and guns, hunting and shooting are much less commonplace. Too many people have become afraid of guns.

But guns are just tools. Use any tool, from a hammer to a lawn mower, the wrong way and it can become dangerous. No one has a problem with chain saws, but no one would use a chain saw to carve the Thanksgiving turkey, either.

The same thing is true for guns. They're not toys. They don't belong in school. They shouldn't be used to settle arguments.

Fear of guns is rooted in ignorance. These books are intended to replace fear and ignorance with knowledge. A youngster who absorbs *The Gun Book for Boys* will have a grasp of shooting fundamentals that few adults do; and an involved parent who backs up that youngster with what's in this book will understand what's going on.

But don't just take our word for it. Karim Baker and Lisa Mayers are two suburban mothers who went through what you may be facing right now. They and their young sons, Hayden and Chris, gave us input on both of these books. You should hear from them directly.

❖

KID-TESTED AND MOTHER-APPROVED

Steve Helsley

Karim Baker and son Hayden (holding his GSG-1911 .22 pistol; note trigger-finger position and open action). "We come from a family that was not involved in shooting in any way."

Karim: For me, one of the most challenging moments as a parent proved to be coping with a son who decided that guns had become his true passion. I'm not even sure how this happened, as we come from a family that was not involved in shooting in any way. Naturally, this put me (and my husband) at a huge disadvantage when it came to guiding a 14-year-old in the right direction in his new hobby. Unfortunately, we adults cannot claim ignorance when it comes to our children's safety. Knowledge, as they say, is power, and so the quest for information about guns became my new undertaking.

The Gun Book for Boys is a parent-friendly/child-friendly user's guide. It is a thorough introduction for kids who are interested in firearms as well as for adults who are new to the gun world. Not only does this book explain the who, what, when, where and how of firearms, but it also incorporates considerable history, not to mention some good fact-checking and true-story telling.

Lisa: I, on the other hand, come from a family of card-carrying gun nuts. With a dad and grandpa who are very knowledgeable and experienced shooters, with backgrounds in law-enforcement, ballistics, hunting and long-range rifle competition, my 13-year-old son and his older sister have had the opportunity to learn about guns and to shoot since childhood. Since early childhood, in fact—under close and expert supervision, naturally. Our local range has proven to be another wonderful resource for firearms instruction, as it offers shotgun and rifle training for young people.

For those who don't have these advantages or who would like to build on what they already know, our family members all agree that *The Gun Book for Boys* is a great guide. Karim and I both appreciated the chance to read drafts of it and to contribute to it.

As moms, we both have seen some very positive changes in our sons since they discovered the world of firearms and shooting. They have become much more thoughtful and mature, which for teenagers is a small miracle! Much of this appears to have been a result of understanding the risks and responsibilities that go with owning and using firearms.

Both of our boys are developing greater self-confidence as they become more skilled in their shooting, and it is a delight to see their passion and understanding grow as they inhale the history behind the guns that they are exposed to. The knowledge that they absorb like sponges continues to amaze us. Neither of us will be surprised if our boys choose careers that somehow involve firearms. And even that is addressed in this book.

Parents, if you're looking for a surefire way to arm your child with an understanding of firearms and shooting in a thorough yet entertaining way, *The Gun Book for Boys* hits the target.

Lisa Mayers and son Chris (holding his Remington Model 514 .22 rifle; note trigger-finger position and open action). "I, on the other hand, come from a family of card-carrying gun nuts." Note the cast on Chris' left wrist—broken while skiing, which kept him from shooting. See "Information About Guns, Shooting & Safety."

Steve Helsley

This book is intended not only for parents who have little or no background in shooting, but also for those who have some shooting knowledge and want to ensure that their children receive a thorough and proper introduction to guns. Any responsible parent naturally has concerns about the safe use of firearms, and we mean to address those concerns. Perhaps in the process we can also open some eyes to the reality of the shooting sports, free from political or philosophical wrangling.

Reading the following chapters in order should answer your questions in logical sequence, but you can also use this book as a sort of operator's manual. As you and your youngster feel your way into shooting, go back to the table of contents for areas of particular concern, and read and re-read as needed.

As you perhaps already know, there is also a vast (and constantly growing) archive of information about every aspect of guns and shooting online. This can be extremely useful but also overwhelming and even intimidating. Much of the Internet lacks "adult supervision," so it can be difficult to separate right from wrong and correct from incorrect information. But if you use this book as a foundation and a springboard and your youngster absorbs *The Gun Book for Boys*, together you can't go far wrong.

Silvio Calabi
Steve Helsley
Roger Sanger

Information About Guns, Shooting & Safety

Truths, Half-Truths & Misconceptions About Gun Ownership and Use

WHAT IS IT WITH AMERICA AND GUNS?

Modern American history began in 1607 with the arrival of 500 English colonists at Jamestown Plantation, in what is now Virginia. They brought guns to help ensure their survival in the wilderness. Thirteen years later and 500 miles to the northeast, another shipload of English settlers established Plymouth Plantation. They too were well armed and, by 1630, the Massachusetts Bay Colony required that all men, including servants, be "furnished with good & sufficient armes" and would provide guns to those who couldn't afford them.

America was settled by Europeans just as firearms were evolving from unreliable curiosities to functional tools. This may not have been a coincidence. The first Europeans known to have reached North America were Vikings who arrived in Newfoundland around AD 1000. Their settlement failed. Some historians suspect the Norsemen were driven away because their swords, axes and bows provided little or no advantage over the natives' weapons. The English adventurers and Pilgrims who arrived 400 years later had guns and were able to defeat the Indians and stay. In a sense, America and firearms grew up together.

The National Firearms Museum

One of America's first guns: The wheellock rifle attributed to John Alden, one of the founders of what became the Massachusetts Bay Colony. Legend has it that he was the first to step onto Plymouth Rock when the *Mayflower* arrived in the New World in 1620. Alden, who lived until 1687, became a high-ranking official in the colonial administration, which may explain how a one-time carpenter could own such an expensive Italian-made weapon. The rifle was found in a hidden compartment in the Alden home when the home was being restored in 1924. The house survived the centuries without being destroyed by fire, a common fate in early America.

America became the United States of America during the Revolution. The conflict began with shots fired on April 19, 1775, when British troops marched out of Boston to seize colonists' guns and ammunition. Americans have been a bit touchy about this subject ever since.

That was less than 250 years ago—just an eyeblink in human history. For most of those two-plus centuries, much of America remained a raw land where guns put meat on the table, protected against Indians and outlaws, and enabled families to put down roots, commerce to prosper and the nation to grow and defend itself. As civilization spread across the North American wilderness, the notion of taking such essential tools as guns away from law-abiding citizens was simply unthinkable.

In June 2010 the Supreme Court ruled that owning guns is one of America's Constitutional rights.

HOW MANY GUNS ARE THERE IN AMERICA?

The first official US census took place in 1790, seven years after the Revolution ended, and determined that 3,929,214 "free White males of 16 years and upward, free White males under 16 years, free White females, all other free persons (by sex and color), and slaves" lived in America. This probably meant upward of 650,000 households, nine-tenths of which were involved in farming. It's likely that each of these families had at least one gun. Much of the rest of America's white male population probably also had guns, even if only pocket pistols kept in nightstands in houses in Boston, New York or Philadelphia.

Since then, the number of firearms (civilian, police and military) in the US has grown to approximately 300 million, of which about 100 million are handguns. More are added every year.

Survey data from 2010 suggests that 47 to 53 million American households (40 to 45 percent) have at least one firearm. Of these households, 67 percent own a gun for self-protection, 66 percent for target shooting and 42 percent for hunting.

Bottom line: If you're concerned about the "proliferation" of guns in our country, it's too late; they proliferated centuries ago.

But we're not here to debate gun control. Our goal is to guide and inform parents whose children are interested in the shooting sports.

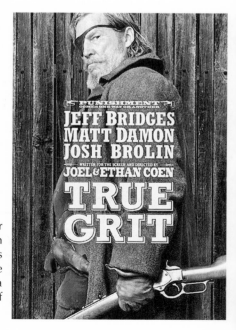

Don't discount the impact of guns on popular culture—or of American pop culture on gun ownership and shooting. These two movies were released 60 years apart. The first feature film ever made in Hollywood, in 1914, was a western called *The Squaw Man*, with plenty of cowboys, Indians and guns.

Isn't It Dangerous to Have a Gun at Home?

According to the National Safety Council, in 2009 there were 600 accidental shooting deaths in the United States. This is a 60-percent decrease since 1989, when there were 1,489 such fatalities, and an 81-percent reduction since 1929, when there were 3,200 such deaths—even though the US population was only 40 percent of what it is now.

In 2009 the 600 deaths amounted to 0.6 percent of all accidental deaths, or six of every 1,000. Of these 600 people accidentally killed by firearms, 59 were children aged 14 or younger.

For perspective: In 2009 the leading causes of accidental death at home were poisoning (34,300), falls (16,900), fire (2,900), choking (2,300), mechanical suffocation (1,500), drowning (1,100) and "natural heat and cold" (500).

Four hundred of the 600 accidental firearms fatalities occurred at home. Outside the home, motor vehicles were the leading cause of accidental deaths in America in 2009: 35,900.

(These statistics were published by the National Safety Council in 2011, with the caveat that the figures were still preliminary, even though they were from '09. Evidently, it takes a long time to crunch the numbers.)

It's no accident (indeed) that the firearms death rate is so low. If you read or even just skim this book or *The Gun Book for Boys*, you will get a sense of how seriously shooters take safety and how many organizations foster and teach safe gun-handling.

To cite just two of the support groups listed at the back of this book: Since 1988 the National Rifle Association has presented its highly regarded Eddie Eagle GunSafe Program to 25 million kindergarten through third-grade children, and the National Shooting Sports Foundation's Project ChildSafe has provided more than 35 million gun-safety kits to Americans at no charge.

* ⫯⫯ ⊠⫯ *

What About Hunting? Isn't That Dangerous?

Research suggests that hunting is one of the safest of all outdoor activities. According to IHEA, the International Hunter Education Association, in 2010 the 16,300,000 licensed firearms hunters in America suffered 8,122 injuries. The great majority of these were non-fatal and unrelated to guns.

That's a rate of 0.05 percent, or one injury per every 2,000 hunters. This is more injuries than occurred playing billiards or pool (one for every 5,314 players) but less than bowling, where one of every 1,607 people got hurt enough to become a statistic. The most dangerous sport or

recreational activity by far is football, which in 2010 recorded an injury for every 19 participants.

(These numbers are complied from data collected by the US Fish and Wildlife Service, the National Sporting Goods Association, the Consumer Products Safety Commission and the National Electronic Injury Surveillance System.)

Again, this extremely low accident rate is no accident. For more than 50 years IHEA, a professional association of 67 state and provincial wildlife conservation agencies, with the assistance of 70,000 volunteer instructors, has taught hunter safety to more than 750,000 people each year in the US. Overall, since 1949 more than 35 million people in America have received such training in firearms safety and the elements of responsible hunting.

If you're also concerned about the ethics of killing wild animals, please see "Hunting," elsewhere in this book.

KEEPING AN OPEN MIND

*P*erhaps you've heard the saying that "there are lies, damn lies and statistics"? We encourage you to do your own research on safety and any other issues presented in this book and in *The Gun Book for Boys*. The Internet makes this easier than ever before, but it demands a discriminating eye. Anyone can post anything online at any time, so be aware of your sources.

Be especially critical of statistics about children and guns. Look closely at what is meant by "child" or "teen" or even "young person." The accepted age for a child is 14 or younger, but some conflated statistics bump that up to 19 or even into the early twenties. This lets the accidental death of a 6-year-old be grouped statistically with that of a street-gang member killed by police during a crime.

FACTS & FIGURES

Firearms are Involved in Less Than 1.5 Percent of Unintentional Fatalities among Children

For children and youth 14 years of age and under, unintentional injuries are the leading cause of fatality. **But firearms account for the lowest cause of injury among youth.**

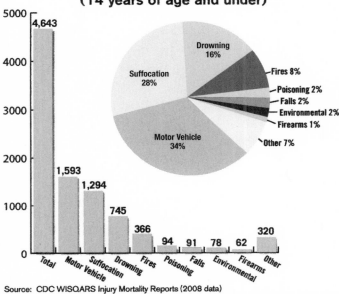

Unintentional Fatalities:
(14 years of age and under)

Source: CDC WISQARS Injury Mortality Reports (2008 data)

Firearms are Involved in Fewer Than 1 Percent of All Unintentional Fatalities

TOTAL U.S. POPULATION 304,374,846		
Total Unintentional Fatalities	**121,902**	**100%**
Motor Vehicle	37,985	31.2%
Poisoning	31,116	25.5%
Falls	24,013	19.7%
Suffocation	6,125	5.0%
Drowning	3,548	2.9%
Fires, Flames & Smoke	2,992	2.5%
Natural / Environmental	1,409	1.2%
Transportation (other than land)	981	0.8%
Struck By / Against Object	891	0.7%
Machinery	693	0.6%
Firearms	592	0.5%
All Other Accidents	11,557	9.4%

Source: CDC WISQARS Injury Mortality Reports (2008 data)

Firearm-related Fatalities among Youth Down 78 Percent

Over the last two decades the number of unintentional firearm-related fatalities among youth 14 years of age and under **decreased by 78 percent, and by 49 percent in the last 10 years.**

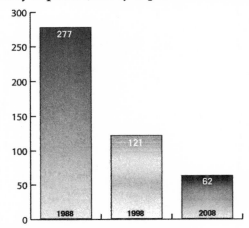

Source: CDC WISQARS Injury Mortality Reports (2008 data)

Historical Flashback

Today, the annual number of unintentional firearm-related fatalities is **down 81 percent** from a high of 3,200 in 1929.

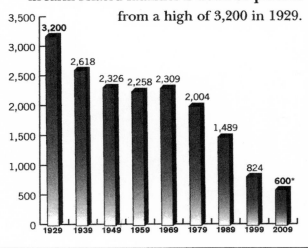

* preliminary
National Safety Council Injury Facts 2011 Edition

National Shooting Sports Foundation

Junior Wants to Shoot! Now What?

Make a Plan with Your Young Shooter

oes your child truly want to become a shooter? Or does he or she just want to try it? At this point, it's worth remembering that many kids have the attention span of a mayfly. Their interests bounce all over the place and often don't last more than a week or so at a time. Males of our generation wanted to be cowboys or firefighters or astronauts; darn few of us stuck to those dreams. When it comes to guns and shooting, your youngster may be on the verge of a lifetime avocation (or even vocation), or he may just be intensely curious. Kids hear of their friends or peers doing something interesting—and what's more interesting than guns and shooting, with that alluring whiff of danger?—and want to do it too.

The surest way to stoke a youngster's interest in something is by declaring it "Completely out of the question" and "Over my dead body!" On the other hand, a willingness to let your kid try shooting may satisfy his or her curiosity, and the interest may simply fizzle out.

The reality of shooting may turn out to be too different from the perception, even if your youngster has devoured *The Gun Book for Boys*. The noise of shooting might be too bothersome. Punching holes in a target may prove to be boring, or trying to break a flying clay target too frustrating. The chores and discipline that go with guns may be too much.

You won't know until you try. Fortunately, that's fairly easy. Most shooting ranges offer

Reality is often different from perception. Test your youngster's interest by letting him or her fire a few shots, properly supervised, at a well-equipped range.

National Shooting Sports Foundation

introductory sessions for prospective shooters—i.e., new members or clients. You can find them online or in the phone book. The National Shooting Sports Foundation has packaged a comprehensive directory of shooting ranges across the US in a smartphone app called Where2Shoot. It's available for free (ages 17 and up) from the Sports category in the iTunes store.

Another tack is to visit the gun department of a large sporting-goods or outdoor store such as Cabela's and simply ask: "My son/daughter would like to try shooting. What do you recommend? Do you have a range?" There are other approaches in the chapter called "Getting Started."

FAMILIARIZE YOURSELF WITH FIREARMS LAWS

So your child has fired an age-appropriate gun under adult supervision, and it's clear that his or her interest is real. Now, assuming that you will support an immersion in this activity, you have to get serious also.

First, there are the legal issues. Firearms laws are especially complex for shooters who are not of legal age—whatever that is. In the US a "minor" is generally defined as a person under 18, the voting age. When it comes to alcohol, however, a minor is someone under the age of 21. And in terms of criminal responsibility, a "juvenile" may be someone under 17—or 16 or only 14. Just as they do for driving a car, laws governing the possession of firearms by minors, juveniles or other "underage" persons vary from state to state.

You can research general state law easily at http://law.findlaw.com/state-laws/. You can find state gun laws at http://www.nraila.org/gun-laws/state-laws/. Or go to www.gunlaws.

com and browse the Bloomfield Press list of books about state gun laws.

However, laws regulating where and even when shooting is allowed often differ from one municipality to another. Your city or town almost certainly has an official Website where you can find bylaws, ordinances and policies that address everything from flea markets to firearms exclusion zones.

If your research leaves you in doubt, call or visit your local police station or a retailer that sells guns and put your questions to them. You'll need to establish a relationship with such a retailer anyway to buy safety gear, ammunition, targets and so on, not to mention a gun(s), and this is an excellent way to begin. (There's much more about this in "Getting Started.")

TAKE RESPONSIBILITY AND SET RULES

Abiding by the law is non-negotiable and necessary, of course, but until your child leaves home to take up his or her own life as an adult, it's best to adopt the attitude that you are responsible for his or her behavior—especially when it comes to guns and shooting.

Parents must set rules about their young shooters' possession of guns and ammunition as well as how, when, where and with whom they shoot. However, you can't set meaningful rules unless you understand what's involved.

After you've read this book, keep it handy as a reference, using the table of contents as a guide. A youngster who's read *The Gun Book for Boys* will know much more about guns and shooting than you do (and more than most adult shooters), but you'll be able to keep up your end of the conversation. You also will know where and when to step in and exert more control.

We recommend "rule by consensus." That is, talk with your young shooter and develop a plan together. Determine what's OK and what's off-limits, and be aware (as if you could forget) that kids change a lot between 12 and 18. Set

goals and rewards that are linked to age, performance in school and other achievements or proficiency: "If you stay on the honor roll and keep your room clean and your mentor says you're ready, on your 14th birthday we'll buy you a .22 rifle." Or whatever. This is a tremendous opportunity to do something meaningful with your child and to be involved in his or her life.

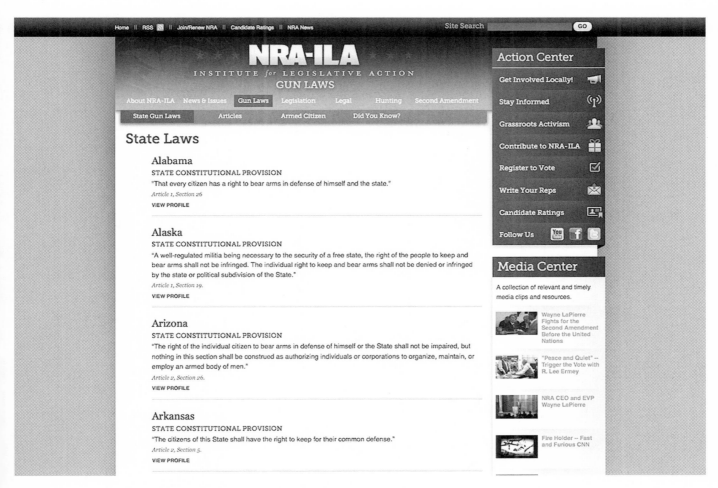

The landing page for state gun laws, at www.nraila.org/gun-laws/state-laws/, on the National Rifle Association's Website. Your city or town probably has a site where you can find bylaws, ordinances and policies that address everything from flea markets to firearms exclusion zones.

Getting Started

Learning to Shoot

Were we, the authors, starting over, with a passion to know about guns and shooting and all that fascinating stuff, we would wish for a trusted advisor to lead us down the path of discovery: Someone we looked up to and who could answer our questions with a blend of experience and knowledge. No doubt you would like the same for your child; and the peace of mind might help you sleep better.

If you are an experienced shooter, you're already ahead of the game and may simply be looking for ways to fine-tune your introductory game plan. If you have no knowledge of guns, you're going to need assistance. Unfortunately, grandfathers who 1) grew up with guns and 2) live nearby are getting scarce. If you live in an urban or suburban environment, neighbors or family friends with experience in shooting are also often in short supply. (Keep in mind, though, that in this day and age many shooters don't talk about what they do, at least until they know that it will get a friendly reception. You'll never know unless you ask.)

When a door closes, a window (or three) opens somewhere else. There was a time when the notion of taking classes to learn to shoot would have been distinctly odd, at least in America. Family and friends taught kids how to handle guns. Today conservation groups, state fish and

The course materials for the Boy Scouts of America's merit badges in rifle and shotgun shooting are two of the very best instructional books available.

game departments, youth organizations, outdoor clubs, gun companies, sporting-goods retailers and shooting ranges have filled the family-and-friends vacuum with a wide range of available shooting instruction. Entry-level courses not only get your youngster off to a secure start, but also can help you find a mentor for him or her.

HUNTER-SAFETY COURSES

The least-expensive shooting-related instruction is often the approved hunter-safety course that every state requires a new hunter to pass before it will issue him or her a license. This will provide a basic understanding of firearms and their maintenance, ammunition, shooting skills, safe hunting practices, hunting ethics and first aid in the field. It also will begin to drum into students' heads the rules of firearm safety.

This will again test your child's resolve and interest. You may say, for example, "Take this course and see how you like it. If you do well, then we can talk about getting you into shooting." It will also introduce your child—and you, when you pick up and drop off—to a number of adult shooters, many of whom are genuinely glad to help newcomers. Making such a connection can take nothing more than asking for extra help from one of the instructors. These people are almost always volunteers, by the way.

State-sanctioned hunter-safety courses typically last 12 to 20 hours spread out over several weeks, and there may be a nominal fee. There is usually no minimum age requirement, but children younger than about 10 seldom have the strength or arm length to safely manage even small-caliber rifles or shotguns. The courses end with practical and written tests. Passing grades earn a Hunter Safety Certificate, which entitles the bearer to buy a hunting license in any state. (Most states, however, won't sell a firearms hunting license to anyone younger than 12 or so, and then may limit them to hunting with licensed adults until they reach a certain age.)

Go online and search for "hunter safety course" for your state. You'll find that many states now teach at least parts of these courses over the Internet, but you'll want your child to learn hands-on and to rub shoulders with prospective mentors.

A number of national conservation and outdoor associations have created their own young-hunter programs. These range from 4-H clubs (www.4-hshootingsports.org) to the Rocky Mountain Elk Foundation (www.rmef.org) and the National Wild Turkey Federation (www. nwrg.org/jakes).

NOT INTERESTED IN HUNTING?

If you or your child are not interested in hunting, there is another way: a shooting range or club. (FYI, there is an extensive section on hunting in *The Gun Book for Boys*.)

In a rural area this might be a fish & game club where members go to sight in their deer rifles and shoot a few rounds of trap or skeet with their bird guns. But if you live in or near a city, you may be surprised at how many duly certified and sophisticated shooting facilities you'll find—parcels of land well equipped for a variety of rifle, pistol and/or shotgun sports, or indoor ranges set up for target shooting. Some of these are associations with membership dues; others are for-profit commercial enterprises that charge fees. Some have retail stores attached that sell everything from ammunition and targets to guns, clothing and all the associated gear.

Virtually all of these operations offer instruction, often at levels that extend from basic firearms skills to Olympic-level shooting disciplines. All of them stress safety and responsible behavior with firearms. All of them look for new members or customers, too, and offer programs to bring newcomers into the fold. Young shooters are particularly welcome, and mentor candidates are usually plentiful. (Many older, experienced shooters are frustrated because their own children or grandchildren aren't interested in the sport.)

If you can't find a range or club on the Internet, go to a sporting-goods store or gun-shop and ask where their clients shoot. Local police departments usually have a vested interest in seeing their citizenry able to handle firearms safely, and they may have some helpful advice.

The Boy Scouts of America offers merit badges for shotgun and rifle shooting and has developed outstanding course materials for this. Furthermore, a Scout merit-badge counselor or an older boy, perhaps an Eagle Scout, could become a mentor. The Girl Scouts has no such nationwide programs, but individual Girl Scout troops have created their own shooting courses with the help of NRA-certified instructors.

The NRA (National Rifle Association of America) offers a huge range of firearms training opportunities, including basic instruction. (This is what the NRA was founded to do, back in 1871.) Again this is a fine way to give a youngster a safe start in shooting and fertile ground for mentor candidates.

Many of these nonprofit instructional programs rely on the commercial or association shooting ranges mentioned earlier, so you may see some overlap in these recommendations.

The National Shooting Sports Foundation has an introductory program called First Shots, which tours the country (www.nssf.org/first-shots). The American Legion has a Junior Shooting Sports Program (www.legion.org/shooting). The United States Olympic Team has a Junior Olympic Shooting Program (www.usashooting.org). Even the US government teaches shooting through its Civilian Marksmanship Program (www.odcmp.org), chartered in 1903.

One of the largest gun companies in the US is Daisy, the venerable maker of BB and pellet guns. For many decades most American shooters started with a Daisy, a fact that the company has capitalized on by creating its own array of shooting curricula, safety rules, books and competitions (daisy.com/education.html). As well, most of the outdoor sporting-goods chains—Cabela's, Bass Pro Shops, Sportsman's Warehouse and others—periodically offer coaching to new shooters.

There is a summary of this information in the chapter called "Youth Programs in the Shooting Sports."

FINDING A MENTOR

No introductory shooting course will magically bestow sound judgment, depth of knowledge or even common sense on a 13-year-old. It will whet (or possibly extinguish) his or her appetite for guns and shooting, and it may impart just enough knowledge to be dangerous. A neophyte shooter should emerge from such a course directly into the arms of the trusted advisor we mentioned earlier.

The ideal shooting mentor makes safety the first priority, followed by fun, and this usually means lots of supervised shooting of age-appropriate guns. Some adults think it's amusing to hand an inexperienced kid a 12-gauge shotgun or a big-bore handgun and watch him or her deal with the blast and the recoil. At the very least, this is scary; at the worst, it's dangerous. It certainly won't put your child on the path to shooting happiness.

A mentor needn't be able to answer every question about guns—most shooters don't know much about the transitions between flintlock, percussion, needlefire, pinfire and centerfire ignition, or whether a special-ops warrior really can fire a Minigun from the hip, like Jesse Ventura in *Predator*—but he should know how to find the answers. He or she should also have enough technical background to know what's safe or practical and what isn't. "Hey, can you fire a marble out of a 20-gauge shotgun? Why not?" (Wikipedia and Google offer a lot of answers, but not necessarily the right ones.)

As teacher and, inevitably, role model, a mentor assumes responsibility for your child's safety, at least part-time. A mentor is also responsible to you, the parent, and you must establish an effective working relationship. You must be kept up to date on all activities, and you must be able to say yes or no.

And then, naturally, a mentor needs insight and understanding, sympathy, generosity, patience and a willingness to be helpful. A well-stocked gun safe and shooting library don't hurt, either.

Steve Helsley

Every new shooter should have an experienced (insightful, understanding, sympathetic, generous, patient and helpful) mentor. As teacher and role model, a mentor assumes responsibility for your child's safety, at least part-time, and you must establish an effective working relationship with him or her. (This mentor is about to tell his student to get her face properly down onto the gun stock.)

Gun Basics

Knowledge Is Power

Like every activity, shooting has its own vocabulary, and you can't understand the sport—or communicate with your young shooter—without a grasp of basic terminology. *The Gun Book for Boys* has a comprehensive glossary in the chapters "Talking the Talk" and "Guns, Guns, Guns," but this chapter will give you your own working knowledge of guns and ammunition, and it ends with some guidance on how to handle them. We've also included our perspective on two popular shooting games, Paintball and Airsoft, although your youngster may not appreciate it.

A **firearm** is a gun that launches a projectile through the action of an explosive: the gunpowder in the ammunition. Technically, a **BB gun** or a **pellet gun** is not a firearm because it's powered by compressed air or some other gas. Collectively, the latter two are called air guns.

Federal law and most state laws treat firearms and air guns as two different things. But some towns and cities define "firearm" as something like "any instrument used in the propulsion of pellets, shot, shells or bullets by action of gunpowder, compressed air or gas exploded or released within it." The definitions are important, because it's illegal to discharge a firearm within most municipalities. This means that, depending on where you live, your youngster could get into legal trouble even with a BB gun, not just a true firearm.

(The word "gun" itself can be confusing. It actually means a shotgun, not a rifle or a pistol, but it's widely applied to all sorts of firearms and air guns.)

The power of different guns (or the cartridges they shoot) varies enormously. Naturally, the more powerful a gun is—in other words, the larger the projectile and the faster and farther it goes—the more dangerous it can be, but even low-powered guns can cause serious damage and have to be treated with respect.

Most youngsters can't manage the weight, noise and recoil of high-powered guns, but even the least-powerful true firearm, a .22 rimfire, can propel its bullet nearly a mile.

People have even been killed with BB or pellet guns that unsuspecting users have dismissed as toys. Air guns are far less powerful than even .22 rimfires, but they are emphatically not toys.

Air-gun pellets (left) are generally made of lead and have an aerodynamic shape. BBs are simply round balls, usually copper-plated steel. Bullets (top center) are usually lead, with or without some sort of coating.

Steve Helsley

A **BB** is a tiny round ball (.177 caliber—4.5mm in diameter, or less than one-sixth of an inch) usually of copper-plated steel. A **pellet** is a lead projectile, usually .22 or .177 caliber, with an aerodynamic cone-shaped head. "Caliber" is explained below, but it just means diameter.

A **rifle** fires a single projectile—a bullet. "Rifle" comes from "rifling," the half-dozen or so grooves cut along the inside of the barrel, or **bore**, in long spirals. The bullet is a tight fit in the bore; the rifling grips the bullet and makes it spin in the air, so it flies more accurately.

To be clear: An air gun may or may not be a rifle; that is, it may or may not have rifling in its barrel. Inexpensive BB guns generally are "smoothbores"—no rifling. More expensive, higher-performance air guns that fire pellets for hunting or competition generally do have rifled barrels.

Shotguns also are smoothbores; more on them later.

Air Guns. This is what many young shooters start with. There are three kinds. The first two, spring-air and pneumatic, are powered by air compressed

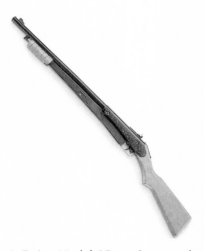

A Daisy Model 25, an inexpensive pump-action spring-air-type BB gun meant for kids. But it's not a toy and it demands supervision, or at least rules.

by the shooter. BB guns are the spring-air type: Cocking them (usually with a lever) compresses a spring, which when it is released (by pulling the trigger) pushes a piston that creates a blast of air to shove the BB down the barrel. Most spring-air BB guns are sized for kids and have springs soft enough for them to compress.

Spring-air pellet guns, on the other hand, are usually for adults and have different cocking mechanisms and stiffer springs.

Pneumatic air guns have to be pumped repeatedly with a lever or a handle, which raises the pressure in the air cylinder, inside, that powers

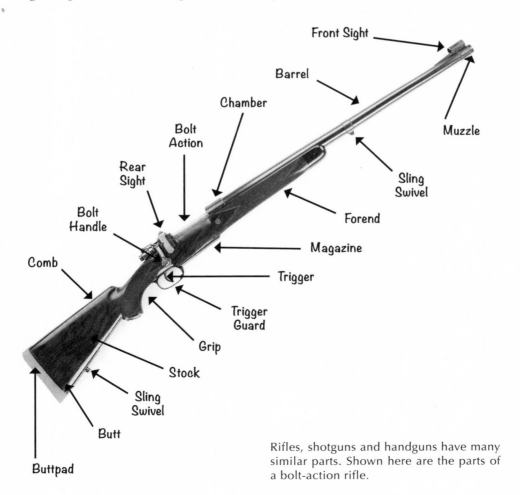

Rifles, shotguns and handguns have many similar parts. Shown here are the parts of a bolt-action rifle.

A high-powered adult spring-air pellet rifle made by Gamo for target shooting and small-game hunting.

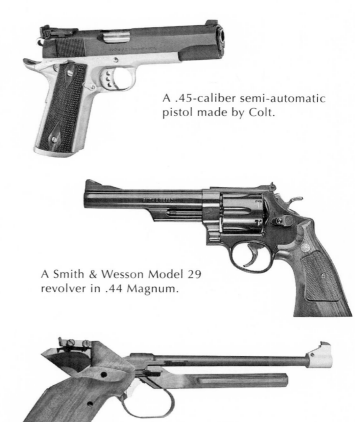

A .45-caliber semi-automatic pistol made by Colt.

A Smith & Wesson Model 29 revolver in .44 Magnum.

A Swiss-made Hämmerli .22-caliber single-shot target pistol.

the piston that fires the BB or pellet. More pumping increases the pressure and thus the velocity and power of the projectile.

The third kind of air gun is that powered by compressed CO_2, carbon dioxide. This saves having to pump, but it means buying gas cylinders. Even the small 12-gram cylinders that fit into a pistol have enough charge to fire dozens of rounds. If the gun is put away before the charge is used up, the leftover gas will eventually leak out; meanwhile, the gun can be fired just by loading a pellet into it.

Some gas-powered guns—Paintball guns, for example—have large built-in gas reservoirs that last much longer and can be refilled.

In 1950 the National Rifle Association established a Junior Qualification Course for air guns as a way to teach firearms safety, and in 1984 air rifles entered Olympic competition. As a result, the power, accuracy and sophistication of air guns have increased tremendously. But the Daisy company still sells a lot of inexpensive, low-powered spring-air BB guns. These are excellent for teaching youngsters shooting basics, but again, they're not harmless toys.

Handguns fire single bullets too, and they generally have rifled barrels. There are three types of handguns: revolvers, semi-automatics and single-shots (see photos). "Pistol" is like "gun"—the word is used for all sorts of handguns, but specifically it means a semi-auto or a single-shot. Being usually less powerful and accurate than rifles, handguns are mostly for plinking (fun shooting), target shooting or self-defense at close range.

There are air- and gas-powered handguns, too, that fire BBs or pellets and may or may not have rifled barrels.

The **caliber** of a rifle or handgun is the diameter of its projectile, which is also the diameter of its bore, the inside of the barrel. This is usually written in millimeters for European guns (9mm, for example) and in decimal fractions of an inch (.308, for example) for American and British guns.

But what a cartridge is called and the diameter of its bullet aren't always the same. Sometimes this is because of the way they're measured, and sometimes it's because gun companies pick certain numbers because they sound good or they're bigger than their competitors'.

It's important to know that the word "caliber" is often used to mean "cartridge." If someone asks, "Hey, what caliber is that rifle?" and the

Steve Helsley

An assortment of "factory" rifle and handgun ammunition, commercially made to exact specifications and tolerances to fit specific guns manufactured to equally stringent standards. The labels tell all.

Cartridges come in a fantastic array of sizes and shapes. Some were developed more than 100 years ago but are still in everyday use.

reply is, "Three hundred," you have to ask again: "Which .300?" It could be a .300 Winchester Magnum, a .300 Weatherby Magnum or any of several other proprietary .300-caliber cartridges, none of which are interchangeable. The shape and weight of their bullets vary, and their cases have different dimensions and hold different amounts of gunpowder. A .300 Winchester Magnum rifle won't fire a .300 Weatherby Magnum round. ("Magnum," by the way, just means "more powerful.")

European metric cartridges usually don't have makers' names attached to them, so they're differentiated by adding a second number, which is the length of the cartridge case: 7.62x22mm, for example. Just to make things more confusing, a few metric cartridges also have English names. For example, the 7.65x17mm Browning is the same as the .32 ACP (Automatic Colt Pistol).

There are many more names and designations, but never mind. The important thing is that these names let us identify so-called factory loads. This means the cartridges are manufactured to precise standards, and we can buy them over the counter and know that one brand of ammunition will fit another company's guns—if they're exactly the same caliber/cartridge.

Cartridges are single units of ammunition, also called rounds. A cartridge has four main components: a projectile; a case, or shell; gunpowder

and a primer. A primer is a tiny igniter in the base of the cartridge that is struck by the gun's firing pin in order to light the gunpowder, which drives the projectile down the barrel.

If the primer is inside the rim of the case (like most .22 ammunition), it's called a rimfire cartridge. More powerful ammunition has a separate primer set into the center of the base of the shell. This is called centerfire ammunition, and these cases can be reloaded and reused.

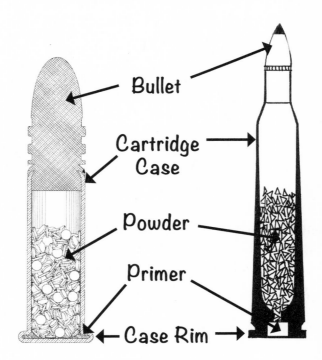

Cutaway drawings of rimfire (left) and centerfire rifle/handgun cartridges, showing the various components. These are not to scale; rimfire cartridges are generally much smaller than centerfire.

A cartridge must fit precisely into the chamber, which is the first section of the gun barrel. (If it doesn't, there's a problem. Stop!)

After firing, the empty cartridge case has to be removed (mechanically or by hand) before the chamber can be reloaded for the next shot.

BB and pellet guns don't fire cartridges because they don't require gunpowder, just the compressed air or gas held in a reservoir somewhere in the gun.

A **bullet** is the projectile, not the entire cartridge. (It's incorrect to say, "I'm out of bullets!" when you're out of ammunition. You're out of cartridges.) The construction and shape of a bullet depends on what it's meant to be shot at—a paper target, a game animal, an enemy fighter and so on. Nearly all cartridges are available with different weights and types of bullets for different uses.

Bullets in assorted sizes and shapes. Left to right: A 450-grain .500-caliber soft-nosed (for expansion) big-game hunting bullet; an entire .22 Long Rifle cartridge (the bullet weighs 40 grains); a 55-grain bullet from a .223 Remington cartridge, also soft-nosed; and a non-expanding 168-grain .308-caliber machine-gun bullet with a tapered base and a full metal jacket.

Bullet weights are given in grains. There are 7,000 grains in a pound, so a 450-grain bullet weighs almost exactly one ounce. Most bullets are less massive than this, however. A .22 bullet may weigh only 40 grains. The standard 5.56mm NATO military rifle bullet weighs 62 grains. Most hunting bullets meant for medium-size game such as deer weigh 120 to 180 grains.

Depending on the caliber/cartridge, bullets are traveling at anywhere from about 1,000 to as much as 4,000 feet per second (fps) when they emerge from the muzzle of a gun. A bullet immediately starts to slow down (because of air resistance) and drop (because of gravity) when it leaves the gun, so it travels along a downward arc called the trajectory. The sights on the gun barrel are adjusted to tilt the barrel upward to compensate for this trajectory. The greater the distance to the target, the higher the rear sight has to be set, because the farther the bullet will drop.

A typical high-powered .30-caliber bullet of, say, 165 grains might leave the rifle at 2,800 fps with 3,200 foot-pounds of energy. By contrast, a .22 rifle fires a 40-grain bullet at 1,100 fps, generating about 105 foot-pounds of energy at the muzzle. This sounds negligible by comparison, but even at 500 yards—more than a quarter-mile—a little .22 bullet can wound or kill.

Guns that fire single projectiles—BBs, pellets or bullets—need **sights** for aiming. Most shooters today use scopes, short for telescopic sights. These are tubes filled with lenses that make the target appear closer. The optics are described as, for example, 4X, which means four times magnification. There are also adjustable models: a 2.5X-to-12X scope can magnify its field of view

Steve Helsley

The lenses in these telescopic rifle sights make the target appear much closer, and thus easier to hit.

from 2½ times to 12 times at the twist of a dial. Inside the scope are crosshairs, a post, a dot or some other kind of reticle—the thing the shooter lays onto the target to aim the gun.

Scopes are rigidly mounted on the gun's receiver and have to be adjusted ("sighted in") for each particular gun and cartridge at a certain distance. A scope set to put a bullet onto a target at 100 yards has to be raised a bit to hit a target that's 200 yards away, because the bullet drops farther at the longer range. The scope can be adjusted mechanically to do this, but in the field a shooter normally just aims a bit higher.

"Open," or "iron," sights have no optics or magnification. To aim, the shooter aligns the front sight, called a bead, with the rear sight, which might be a simple notch or ring. Open sights have to be precisely adjusted for each gun and cartridge also, but beyond about 300 yards even an expert is hard-pressed to hit a small target without the magnification of a scope.

Trained military snipers with special rifles, ammunition and scopes can routinely hit man-size targets at 1,500 yards, and the current sniper record was set in Afghanistan in November 2009 by a British soldier: 2,707 yards—1.53 miles. Incredible.

Shooting well with open sights requires more skill and experience than shooting with a scope, so we advise youngsters to start with them. In *The Gun Book for Boys* we compare it to learning to drive a car with a manual transmission and a clutch. It may never have to be done again, but it's nice to know how—and it makes a youngster a better driver, and shooter. This saves some money, too, as scopes often cost as much as a gun.

Combat pistols and submachine guns (see below) sometimes are equipped with battery-powered laser sights. These project an aiming dot—it's the end of the laser beam—right onto the target. But their range is limited, so they're useful only for close-in shooting.

A **magazine** is the container in a repeating gun that holds the ammunition. A magazine has a spring in it that pushes the cartridges along to where the action (mechanism) of the gun can grab each fresh one and feed it into the chamber for firing.

A magazine ready to be slid into the grip of a Glock pistol. The pistol's slide has been pulled back, ready for loading and cocking.

Rifle and shotgun magazines can be tubes or boxes. A pistol magazine usually slides up into the gun's grip.

A revolver's magazine is the cylinder, here swung out for loading. The cylinder turns (revolves) to align each round with the barrel for firing.

A detachable box magazine removed from its rifle.

Shotgun cartridges that show the range of gauge sizes.

Steve Helsley

Tube magazines usually hold anywhere from a half-dozen to a dozen or more rounds. Box magazines usually hold two to four rounds. Military-style rifles often have long, curved magazines that hold 10 to 30 cartridges. A pistol magazine takes from six to a dozen or more cartridges.

Revolver magazines are called cylinders, which turn (revolve) to bring each cartridge in line with the barrel for firing. Usually they hold six rounds.

A **clip**, by the way, is not a magazine. A clip is a strip of metal that holds a row of cartridges so that they can be slid into a magazine.

Shotguns are, as mentioned, smoothbores; they have no rifling in their barrels (unless they are firing slugs; see below). This is because shotguns fire clusters of pellets, usually lead, that spread out in the air to make it easier to hit a flying target such as a clay pigeon or a gamebird. Because they're generally not fired at static targets, most shotguns don't have rifle-type sights, either. Shotgun shooting is more instinctive than aimed.

Shotguns aren't designated by caliber but by **gauge**. Gauge is the number of equal-size balls that could be made from one

pound of lead that each just fits that-diameter barrel. A 12-gauge gun barrel, for example, would fit a ball that weighs $1/12$ of a pound. A 20-gauge gun is smaller; it would fit a ball that weighs $1/20$ of a pound. We inherited the gauge system from the British, and it's centuries old.

The most common shotgun gauges today are 12 and 20. There are also 10-, 16- and 28-gauge guns and the .410, which is the smallest widely available shotgun. The .410 is a true fractional-inch caliber, not a gauge size. (It's a long story.)

Just as with rifles and handguns, there are many different types and styles of shotguns for target shooting, hunting and tactical use (military, police and self-defense).

The ounce or so of pellets in a typical shotgun cartridge needs a little distance to spread out after it leaves the gun, so inside 20 feet a shotgun blast is highly lethal and destructive, no matter the gauge or whether the gun is loaded with fine

This is a general-purpose, off-the-rack pump-action shotgun made by Browning. It can hold four rounds in its magazine plus one in the chamber.

birdshot or large buckshot. Beyond that distance, the spread of the pellets can be controlled somewhat by "choking" the barrel—shrinking its bore diameter slightly at the muzzle.

Shotguns can also fire single large projectiles called slugs, loaded in special cartridges.

Slugs will kill deer-size game out to about 125 yards or so. Some slugs are grooved to spin in flight, and it is possible to buy rifled barrels with sights for shotguns, but even so slugs don't have the ultimate range and accuracy of bullets.

TYPES OF GUN ACTIONS

Steve Helsley

A lever-action Marlin rifle. Working the lever under the grip back and forth operates the action—ejects an empty shell, re-cocks the hammer and feeds a fresh cartridge into the chamber, ready for firing.

A single-shot rifle made by Ruger. Pushing the underlever forward opens up the action so that it can be loaded, one cartridge at a time.

Single-shot guns fire once and then have to be reloaded and re-cocked. Repeating (multi-shot) guns hold some quantity of ammunition in a magazine and can be fired again more quickly. There are different kinds of repeaters (bolt-action, lever-action, pump-action, autoloading, revolving), but they all require the trigger to be pulled separately for each shot.

A semi-automatic gun reloads and recocks itself; the shooter doesn't have to do anything but pull the trigger once per shot.

A gun that reloads and recocks itself and fires as long as the trigger is held back (until it runs out of ammo) is a full-automatic firearm—a **machine gun**. Civilians can possess and shoot machine guns if they are properly permitted, but machine guns are illegal for hunting.

Full-auto firearms come in all shapes and sizes. A machine pistol is a handgun that can empty its magazine

with just one squeeze of the trigger. A **submachine gun** is a compact, short-range, two-handed machine gun that fires a pistol cartridge. An assault rifle is a full-size, full-auto shoulder weapon for military use that fires a more powerful round. (Read "Meet the AR-15" in "Choosing a First Gun.")

Heavier machine guns are mounted on vehicles (aircraft, trucks, tanks, boats and so on) or fired from stands and served by crews of two or three soldiers.

A submachine gun is a full-auto weapon that fires a pistol cartridge. This is a Heckler & Koch MP5 with a collapsible shoulder stock, a 30-round magazine and a suppressor (silencer) on the barrel.

A word about **reloading**: Many shooters buy cartridge cases, bullets or shot, powder, primers, wads and special tools and create their own ammunition. People who shoot a lot do this to save some money; others do it to try to improve the performance of their guns or because they enjoy it as a hobby. If your youngster becomes interested in reloading, keep this anecdote in mind:

One of the authors was visiting a remote ranch in Montana when a big crew-cab pickup pulled up to the barn and parked. The driver was the 12-year-old son of one of the ranch hands. As the boy got out of the truck, he brought with him a rifle. The back doors opened and three more kids, 4 to 6 years old, got out. The ranch hand saw that the visitor was a bit surprised, so he explained, referring to the driver, "Oh, I never let him drive unless he's armed." Then, as an afterthought, he added, "but he's not old enough for reloading."

Trigger safety. Rule No. 4, below, applies to rifles and shotguns as well as handguns.

Steve Helsley

Certain kinds of shooting do require hand-loaded ammunition, but that's for much later in your youngster's shooting career.

The Cardinal Rules of Gun Safety

1. ALWAYS ASSUME A GUN IS LOADED.

2. NEVER LOAD A GUN UNTIL IT IS TIME TO USE IT.

3. NEVER POINT A GUN AT ANYTHING YOU DON'T WISH TO DESTROY.

4. KEEP YOUR FINGER OFF THE TRIGGER UNTIL YOU ARE READY TO DESTROY YOUR TARGET.

FIREARMS COURTESY

In addition to the safety rules, here are a few things to remember when handling guns:

• When someone shows you a gun, don't just grab it out of the case or off the rack. Ask permission first.

• If a gun is handed to you for inspection and the action is not open, open it—carefully. At all times behave as if the gun is loaded. (If it really *is* loaded and you weren't warned of this, you are officially allowed to make a scene.)

• If you're going to close the action, do this carefully and gently as well. (It is particularly offensive to let the slide on a semi-automatic gun slam shut and to close a break-action gun, like an over/under or side-by-side shotgun, too forcefully.)

• Don't slam the cylinder shut on a revolver; close it manually, and carefully. Don't spin the cylinder, either.

• Take care not to swing the barrel into anything.

• Be aware that a metal belt buckle can scratch a gun.

• Don't operate the action without the owner's permission.

• Don't dry-fire an empty gun (operate the action and pull the trigger) without permission.

• If you wish to look through a scope, make sure the action is open, keep your finger off the trigger, and above all don't point the gun at anyone.

• Never lean a gun up against a wall, a railing, a vehicle and so on without taking care to see that it cannot fall over.

• If you slide a gun into a sleeve or put it in a case, demonstrate (to yourself and anyone with you) that it is unloaded and empty first.

• Whether you're sweaty or not, your skin carries salts. If the bore is big enough to stick your finger into—don't do it. Don't put fingerprints all over the metal exterior of a gun either; if you do, ask for a silicone rag or the like to wipe it down when you're done.

• Return the gun with the action open—in other words, in the condition you should have received it.

AIRSOFT & PAINTBALL: THE DARK SIDE?

Two of the most popular shooting games worldwide are Airsoft and Paintball. To youngsters and young adults, they're like stepping into a video game, but this is exactly why we (and many shooting instructors and organizations) don't like them.

Paintball was born in 1981 as the National Survival Game. The first commercial playing field opened in 1982 in Rochester, New York, and a year later the first national championship took place. Companies sprang up to supply guns, facemasks, body armor and footwear. Paintball is now played indoors and out, informally or with referees and rules and even professional players. Reportedly about 10 million people, mostly males between the ages of 12 and 24, play Paintball in the US.

Paintballs are fat beads of food-grade gelatin. A paintball bursts on impact, so it won't penetrate flesh, but it can leave a welt on bare

The Echo1 USA full-size Gatling-type "Minigun" is one of those Airsoft models that look like real guns that people generally can't own. It weighs 33 pounds, fires thousands of pellets per minute and is driven by an electric motor with a separate power pack. It costs about $3,500.

skin and will destroy an eye. Paintball guns are powered by compressed air or CO_2.

Airsoft is a sort of evolution of Paintball and requires the same sort of closed-off area for team or individual "combat." Airsoft guns fire plastic BBs and are much more sophisticated and expensive than Paintball guns. Airsoft began in Japan, where owning firearms is all but impossible, and then spread to Europe and the US.

About every type of tactical firearm—pistols, submachine guns, assault and sniper rifles, combat shotguns, even grenade launchers and heavy machine guns—is available as an Airsoft replica, often licensed by the maker of the actual gun. You can't tell most Airsoft guns from the real thing until you pick them up, and this is both their great attraction and their fatal flaw. Most of them look like real guns.

In the United States, Airsoft guns must have high-visibility orange tips on their barrels, to set them apart from firearms, but the tips can be removed. There have been some awful instances where police officers felt forced to shoot kids fooling around with what turned out to be Airsoft "toys." A lot of firearms experts think Airsoft is the worst of both worlds: The guns are useless as weapons, but they are so realistic that they can create very dangerous situations.

Our main concern about Paintball and Airsoft is that, like video games, they teach deadly unsafe firearms handling. One of the first rules of shooting is to never point a gun at something or someone you're not willing to kill. Any fan of video war games who has an Airsoft submachine gun can learn everything wrong in a very short time.

Most Paintball and Airsoft players grow up, move on to other hobbies and never handle real guns. Many real shooters, on the other hand, never play these games. They're scared by them and the lessons they can teach.

If your youngster wants to try Paintball or Airsoft . . . you have to decide.

⊷⊱✦⊰⊶

About 10 million people, mostly males between the ages of 12 and 24, play Paintball in the US. Like video games, Paintball and Airsoft teach deadly unsafe firearms-handling. One of the first rules of shooting is to never point a gun at something or someone you're not willing to kill.

Choosing a First Gun

What's It Going to Be? An Important Decision

TYPES OF GUN ACTIONS

There are thousands of guns available for dozens and dozens of different uses that range from plinking ("casual" fun shooting) to big-game hunting, Olympic competition and self-defense. However, for a youngster in the early stages of becoming a shooter, the choice of a first gun narrows drastically. Besides having fun from day one—which calls for minimal noise, recoil and expense and maximal ease of use—the initial goal is to become a safe shooter: to develop the positive habits that carry forward into all kinds of shooting.

The single-shot, break-action, manually cocked H&R "Pardner," a traditional first shotgun—safe, well-made, durable and inexpensive—that's been around for more than a century. There are more examples in the next chapter.

Whether your youngster begins with a rifle, shotgun or handgun, the first question is: What action type? Good safety practices and proper gun-handling techniques are formed by learning methodical, step-by-step procedures. A single-shot gun forces the shooter to stop between shots to remove the empty shell from the chamber, then reload, re-cock, "safe" the action (de-cock it, or engage the safety catch) and aim all over again before disengaging the safety and firing the next round. This breaks down the process of shooting into separate steps and forces the

shooter to think about each one until they become habit.

A semi-automatic gun, however, reloads and re-cocks itself near-instantly, so that the shooter only has to squeeze the trigger to fire again. In this case it's easy for a beginner to become distracted and forget to safe the gun between shots. And if he also forgets muzzle control, the Third Commandment (about where the gun is pointed), with just an inadvertent nudge of the trigger he can put a shot somewhere it wasn't meant to go.

• Whether it fires BBs, pellets or bullets, ideally a first gun should be either a single-shot or a non-automatic repeater such as a pump-, lever- or bolt-action that has to be cycled by hand between shots.

• If it is a repeater, the gun should have a detachable magazine—and it should be detached from the gun. (With tubular magazines, which are built in and cannot be removed, it's easy to forget that rounds are still in the gun.)

• Remember that any repeater (even a semi-auto) can effectively become a single-shot by doling out just one cartridge at a time.

How your youngster learns to shoot can also affect the choice of a first gun. If he or she shoots at a range under the eye of a mentor or coach, a semi-automatic can be OK. Over time, the instructor will (or should) instill the proper safety habits.

HANDGUNS

Many adult women learn to shoot with handguns because their goal is self-defense. (At least one Website is devoted specifically to this: www.myfirstgun.net.) They complete an instruction course, buy a gun, apply for a permit to carry it, and then hope they never have to use it. Well and good, but handguns happen to be fun to shoot, and shooting them well can be extra satisfying because they're more difficult to master than long guns (rifles or shotguns).

However, because they are so compact and the shooter can hold them with just one hand, handguns demand special attention to muzzle control. It's all too easy to wave them around carelessly. If your young shooter has proven himself or herself with a long gun, a handgun can be an appropriate next step. But not the other way around.

Ideally, for all the reasons mentioned above, a young shooter should begin with a small-frame revolver, which has to be cycled by hand, not a semi-automatic pistol.

NOISE & RECOIL

Shooters can learn good safety habits and shooting skills with air guns. What an air gun *doesn't* prepare a beginner for is the noise and recoil of a firearm. The blast can be frightening, and YouTube has plenty of videos of people getting smacked in the face by hard-kicking guns. (A lot of these seem to be unsuspecting novices who were set up by their "friends.") Severe recoil is no joke; it may not cause a direct injury, but it can lead to flinching, which is an involuntary and uncontrollable physical reaction that comes with pulling the trigger.

Recoil affects shooters very differently. Some people are oblivious to it and others, even big macho guys, are almost terrified of it. The suddenness of the accompanying noise may have something to do with this, as people tend to think that suppressed ("silenced") guns don't kick as hard. One way to reduce

Steve Helsley

Here a shooting bench is supporting the weight of the gun—a bolt-action rifle that the youngster is firing, under supervision, one shot at a time. (Note the eye and ear protection.)

the perception of recoil is to wear earplugs inside over-the-ear muffs. (See "Passive Shooting Safety.")

Whether or not they are already comfortable with air-powered guns, new or young shooters should start out with firearms that are chambered for .22 rimfire cartridges, which make a sharp *crack!* but generate essentially no recoil. When a shooter has learned how to hold and fire a gun properly, more powerful cartridges can follow. (Growing a bit in the meantime helps too.) An exception to the .22 rule has to be made for shotguns; see below.

Wingshooting with an appropriately sized smallbore shotgun equipped with a recoil pad. The shooter is wearing eye and ear protection and a vest with a shoulder pad, and she's standing in an enclosure that directs her toward where the clay pigeon will appear.

SHOTGUNS

Some youngsters skip BB guns, .22s and stationary targets and go straight to shooting clay pigeons with shotguns. There's absolutely nothing wrong with this, provided your child has a mentor who understands wingshooting and shotguns. Flying targets that shatter are much more interesting than static paper bull's-eyes or even tin cans.

However, shotguns for youngsters are more problematical than air guns or .22 rifles. It's not just a matter of choosing the smallest-bore shotgun, the .410. Recoil is a function of the mass and velocity of the projectile, and it's possible to pack nearly an adult 12-gauge load of birdshot into even a small .410-bore shotgun. Furthermore, since .410 guns usually weigh a lot less than

12-gauges, there's less mass in the gun to absorb recoil. Thus a .410 loaded with the wrong ammunition can kick uncomfortably hard for a novice.

Conversely, a .410 with light cartridges throws only a small quantity of shot pellets that spread out quickly, so a .410 is effective only at short range. (This is why many people use overloaded cartridges in the .410.) A coach who understands this will lob clay pigeons at slow speeds and easy angles, and with some practice and instruction a novice should soon have little difficulty breaking targets with a .410. There will be more noise and recoil than with a .22 rimfire, but nothing that even a 12-year-old can't handle with proper preparation.

The next step up in bore size is a 28-gauge shotgun. A 28 that fits your young shooter, firing no more than three-quarter-ounce shot loads, should perform very well. All else being equal, it will recoil only a bit harder than a .410—and possibly less, depending on the gun.

However, there's a downside to the .410 and the 28 alike: Cartridges are very expensive.

For this reason alone, many coaches start new shooters with bigger 20-gauge guns or quickly move them up to 20s, which take ammunition that costs only about half as much. Again, if the shot load is appropriate to the weight of the gun and the gun is comfortable for the shooter to ho and is nicely padded at the butt end, the recoil will be very tolerable.

(If your youngster develops a mild bruise on his or her shoulder, don't jump to the conclusion that their shotgun is too powerful. Almost any amount of recoil will cause some bruising, even in adults, especially if they haven't fired a gun in a while.)

Here we'll deviate from our earlier advice about staying away from semi-autos. Because t self-loading mechanism in the gun absorbs som of the recoil energy, a semi-automatic 20-gaug shotgun can be softer-shooting than some .410s and 28s. The key is to find a shotgun of the prop size—and to hand the shooter only one cartridg at a time.

LIKE CLOTHES, GUNS MUST FIT

A rifle or shotgun that is too long or bulky is awkward to hold, and this affects accuracy and muzzle control. The shooter can't bring the gun to his or her shoulder to look down the sights properly. Weight has to be considered also; can the youngster hold it long enough to aim and shoot? Many makers offer shorter guns for kids, and a gun that is sized for a youngster will usually be proportionally lighter, too.

Fit matters when it comes to managing recoil also. A gun with the wrong stock length or shape will seem to recoil harder, or at least more painfully, and it can cause nasty bruising on the shoulder or upper arm and cheek.

Fit is also a concern with handguns, where the diameter of the grip and the overall weight may be a challenge. Junior-size handguns are harder to find today than rifles and shotguns for kids.

Youngsters change dramatically in their teens. A 13-year-old who stands five feet tall needs a relatively lightweight (5- to 7-pound) rifle or shotgun with a short stock, while most 17-year-olds or anyone who stands 5 feet 8 inches or more should be able to handle adult-size guns that weigh up to 10 pounds or so.

The next chapter, "How Much Does It Cos to Shoot?" describes some new guns that are ap propriate for youngsters. A few have adjustable interchangeable stocks that let the gun "grow" with its owner.

All Photos: Steve Helsley

Top: Poor fit. A short stock forces the shooter too far forward on the gun and puts his face close to the exposed hammer.

Bottom: Poor fit. A stock that is too long makes the gun awkward to aim and too muzzle-heavy to hold.

Length of pull, the distance from the trigger to the end of the stock, is especially important for young shooters. When the gun is held in the elbow, like this, the shooter's index finger should comfortably reach the trigger. A youngster's LOP is usually 12 to 13½ inches. This stock is too long.

SECONDHAND STARTER GUNS

Many gunshops sell used rifles, shotguns and handguns. If you can find something suitable, this is an excellent way to get your youngster started at a cost that should be less than buying a new gun. A knowledgeable and ethical retailer should have inspected, cleaned and approved every secondhand gun before it went on display for resale, and he can help you make a selection. With the prospect of a new customer, he may also be motivated to put together a well-priced starter package of a gun and safety lock, ammunition, shooting

National Shooting Sports Foundation

Many retailers include a safety lock with every gun they sell, new or second-hand. This renders a gun inoperable.

glasses, hearing protection, targets, a carrying case and so on. Larger gun stores often have shooting ranges, and a membership or shooting instruction might be part of the package.

Alternatively, many a youngster's first gun is a hand-me-down or a loaner. This too can be a great way to get started, but it could also be completely inappropriate if the gun is too heavy, too long, too powerful or even unsafe. What kind of ammunition does it shoot? Has it been kept up well and is it mechanically sound? If the donor is an experienced shooter, he or she may be able to answer all these questions and more. He also should know better than to offer a gun that's un-

suitable for a novice who's still got some growing to do.

But don't count on it. If you have any doubts or questions about a hand-me-down gun, contact that "knowledgeable and ethical retailer" and ask if he can inspect it. He may charge you a small fee to strip down and examine a gun, but it will be money well spent.

If a used gun seems appropriate but is just too long for your youngster, a gunsmith can shorten the stock and replace the butt pad. Keep the section that was removed; when your child grows six inches next year, it likely can be put back.

There is no market in used BB guns; they're just too inexpensive. Prices for new pellet guns vary from BB-gun levels to thousands of dollars for Olympic-class target guns, so you may find secondhand versions in a gun store. They may not be age-appropriate, though—requiring too much strength to cock or being too long or heavy.

The comments about utility, safety and appropriateness apply to air guns as well as to firearms. When in doubt, consult that retailer or your youngster's shooting mentor.

The secondhand racks can be especially useful when it comes to handguns for young shooters. In the past 25 years, the market has shifted so completely to semi-auto pistols that very few revolvers are still being made in sizes for small hands. However, once upon a time Colt, Harrington & Richardson, Iver Johnson, Smith & Wesson, Astra, High Standard and others made many small-frame .22 revolvers, and these still show up on the used-gun market.

———— ≍◊≍ ————

Meet the AR-15, the 'Modern Sporting Rifle'

Sooner or later your young shooter will probably want a rifle that looks like an AR-15. To some people, this is an "assault weapon" or "black gun" that doesn't belong in civilian hands. The shooting industry, however, calls it the MSR, the Modern Sporting Rifle, and says it's the victim of misinformation. AR-type rifles have become extremely popular in America, and for good reason. Here's the background . . . .

Whether they served in the Civil War, the Indian Wars, the Spanish-American War, World War I or II, Korea, Vietnam, Iraq or Afghanistan, generations of Americans learned to shoot with army rifles. When servicemen returned home, if they went hunting or target shooting, they often did so with what they were most comfortable with: the rifle they'd been trained to use and that they'd come to depend on.

From about 1860 to 1900, Americans' favorite rifles tended to be single-shots or lever-actions. These gave way to the bolt-action rifle, which dominated both world wars and, no surprise, became the standard for civilians too. Then, beginning in the 1950s and based on the US Army's self-loading M1 and M14 rifles, semi-automatics began to get popular at home.

This arc of development led, in the 1960s, to the M16, the rifle that is still issued to US forces today. So far, about 8 million of these have been produced, and it's a rare TV newscast that doesn't show M16s in the hands of American or NATO troops.

"M16" is the military designation for the AR-15, a rifle that was created by a man named Eugene Stoner in the 1950s and produced by the ArmaLite Corporation. ("AR" stands for ArmaLite Rifle, not "assault rifle" or "automatic rifle.")

However, the M16 and the original AR-15 are in fact assault rifles: fully automatic, shoulder-fired military weapons that take a medium-power cartridge. Any full-auto firearm is a machine gun—it runs as long as the trigger is held back and there's ammo in the magazine—and machine guns have been heavily restricted for civilians in the US since 1934. Civilian versions of such rifles fire only semi-automatically, meaning that the trigger has to be pulled separately for each shot.

By now millions of American servicemen and women have been trained to shoot the M16 and a shorter version of it called the M4. In this sense, these guns are no different from the single-shot, bolt-action and semi-auto military rifles of earlier generations, so it's no surprise that civilian counterparts of the M16/M4 have become hugely popular among hunters and target shooters. They are relatively light and easy to carry, rugged, dependable, accurate and, above all, familiar.

This is why the AR-type has been dubbed the "modern sporting rifle." However, it's impossible to tell at a glance whether a particular AR-lookalike is capable of full-auto fire (and therefore a military assault rifle) or if it's a civilian-legal

The "modern sporting rifle" of millions of hunters based on the bolt-action military rifles of two generations ago.

semi-auto rifle. People who aren't aware—or don't care—that there's a difference conflate the two. This led to the political term "assault weapon," which is an enormous bone of contention between pro- and anti-gun lobbyists.

(The M16 and M4 fire the 5.56x45mm NATO round, designed for combat. Semi-automatic civilian AR-type rifles are available chambered for a dozen or more cartridges for different kinds of hunting and target shooting. None of these, by the way, is as powerful as common big-game cartridges used in bolt-action and other kinds of rifles.)

AR-type rifles, or modern sporting rifles, whatever you wish to call them, are legal to own in all 50 states, provided the buyer meets federal, state and local requirements. They're just ordinary semi-autos that happen to look like something else. You can say the same thing about some squirt guns.

The concern you should have about the AR your youngster may want is not what it looks like but that it's a semi-automatic that reloads itself. Until he or she becomes an experienced shooter, it's easy to forget to "safe" the gun (decock it, or at least flip on the safety catch) between shots. And if he or she also forgets about muzzle control—that is, where the gun is pointed—it becomes too easy to put a bullet somewhere it wasn't meant to go. An AR-type is not the ideal beginner's gun.

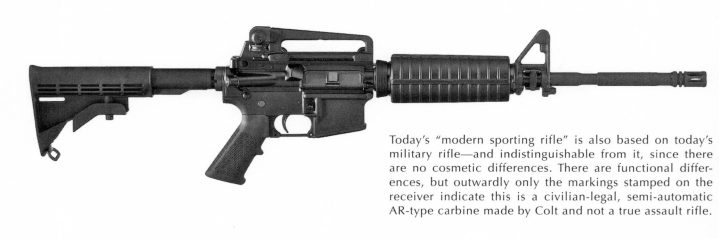

Today's "modern sporting rifle" is also based on today's military rifle—and indistinguishable from it, since there are no cosmetic differences. There are functional differences, but outwardly only the markings stamped on the receiver indicate this is a civilian-legal, semi-automatic AR-type carbine made by Colt and not a true assault rifle.

How Much Does It Cost to Shoot?

A Selection of Guns & Calibers for New Shooters

Most full-line gunmakers offer a few rifles and shotguns that a 12-year-old should be able to handle. Stocks are scaled down and barrels are shorter to reduce the overall weight and improve the guns' balance, the grips are narrower for small hands, and calibers or gauges are age-appropriate in recoil and noise. Any youth shotgun or a rifle of a caliber greater than .22 rimfire should have a soft rubber recoil pad. Many starter guns are single-shots, and some have extra safety features, such as adapters that convert repeaters to single-shot operation or bolts that have to be cocked manually after being closed.

Shown here is a representative selection that includes a BB gun, a pellet gun, a .22 revolver and several types of .22 rifles and small-bore shotguns, all designed for shooters who are less than full-grown—in some cases much less. Also included are several good options for young shooters who are ready to move on to more powerful cartridges, whether for hunting or for target shooting at longer ranges. Prices range from less than $100 to nearly $1,000.

If your youngster is left-handed, your choice may be limited to lever-action, pump-action or break-action guns, as most youth-size bolt-action rifles are designed for right-handed shoot-ers. (Most semi-automatic rifles and shotguns are meant to be cocked with the right hand too.)

Your youngster may already have a gun in mind, and it may not be appropriate for a novice. Ideally, the choice is made by consensus, but of course parents and mentors must have the final approval.

Visit a gunshop or sporting-goods store to inspect and handle any gun before buying it. Is it too heavy? Does it balance well? Does it fit? Does your youngster have the hand strength to open, load, cock and de-cock it easily and safely? Does the trigger work smoothly? If the gun has a safety catch, is it easy to use? Is a trigger lock included? When your shooter outgrows it, will the dealer take it back in trade on something else?

Daisy's Red Ryder Fun Kit: a Red Ryder lever-action BB gun with paper targets, a tin of BBs and kid-size shooting glasses. The gun weighs just a bit more than 2 pounds and is 35 inches long. MSRP is $69.99. A package of 350 BBs should cost no more than $2.

The Benjamin Model 397: a pneumatic .177-caliber pellet rifle. This is a high-quality single-shot that can be pumped as many as eight times to fire pellets at up to 800 feet per second. At 36 inches and 5½ pounds, it's compact but relatively heavy, and a youngster may not be able to pump it to maximum pressure. (Which is not necessarily bad.) MSRP is $179. Pellets cost about $5 for a pack of 250.

 Savage Arms' Rascal bolt-action single-shot .22 rifle is just 31½ inches long and weighs barely 2½ pounds, so holding it up shouldn't be a problem even for a child. It has a high-quality trigger and peepsight, both adjustable. The receiver is drilled and tapped for scope mounts. The stock comes in natural wood or black, green, blue, orange, red, yellow or pink molded synthetic. The bolt can be opened to unload the rifle without pulling the trigger first. MSRP is $213; .22 rimfire ammunition can cost about $8 per 100 rounds—unless it's on sale.

The Henry Mini Bolt is the "official youth rifle" of USA Shooting, the US national team. It's a stainless-steel, single-shot bolt-action that fires .22 Long Rifle or .22 Short cartridges. The adjustable sights have high-visibility fiber-optic inserts. With a black or orange fiberglass stock and a 16¼-inch barrel, the rifle weighs just 3¼ pounds. MSRP is $250. (Henry also makes two lever-action .22 rifles for youngsters with MSRPs of $325 and $515.)

The Marlin Model XT-22 Youth bolt-action rifle is a single-shot .22 with a 12-inch length of pull. With its 16-inch barrel and 33-inch overall length, the rifle weighs 4 pounds. The trigger-pull weight and sights are adjustable, and the receiver is prepped for scope mounts. It is available with a hardwood or synthetic stock and a blued or stainless-steel action and barrel. Some models can accept a detachable seven-shot box magazine. MSRPs are $180 to $200.

The Model 452 Scout from CZ USA is a hefty, wooden-stock bolt-action .22 rifle with a 12-inch length of pull and 16½-inch barrel. At 32¾ inches overall length, it weighs 5 pounds. The trigger pull is adjustable, and the rifle has adjustable buckhorn sights and a dovetail groove for mounting a scope. The Scout comes with a single-shot adapter, but detachable five- or 10-round box magazines are available. MSRP is $303.

The BL-22 Micro from Browning is a top-quality small lever-action .22 repeater that holds up to 15 Long Rifle or 22 Short cartridges in its tubular magazine. With a 12-inch length of pull, a 16¼-inch barrel and an American walnut stock, it weighs 4¾ pounds. The lever needs only a short, 33-degree throw, and the trigger moves with it (so no pinched fingers). The sights are adjustable, and the receiver is grooved for scope mounts. MSRP is $540.

The .22-caliber Ruger New Bearcat, a beautifully made six-shot, at just 24 ounces (1½ pounds) overall and with a 4.2-inch barrel, is one of the few current-production revolvers that comes close to fitting young hands. As a single-action, the gun has to be cocked manually, by pulling back the hammer with the thumb, before it can be fired. MSRP is $549.

The Youth Trifecta set from Rossi USA comes with three easily interchangeable single-shot barrels that are chambered for .22 Long Rifle, 20-gauge shotshells, and either .243 Winchester or .44 Magnum, making it suitable for everything from plinking to target shooting as well as game from woodchucks to turkeys, deer and birds. The rifle barrels have adjustable sights and bases for scope mounts. A removable cheekpiece alters the stock for use as a shotgun or rifle, and the gun comes with a recoil pad, a shoulder sling and a carrying case. The break-open action has several safety fea-tures, including an exposed hammer that has to be cocked manually. With any one of its barrels, the Rossi weighs about 6¼ pounds, so it's suitable for teenagers. MSRP is $329.

(With its mild recoil but excellent perfor-mance, the .243 is a very good starter centerfire car-tridge; ammunition costs about 75¢ per round and up. The .44 Magnum is a revolver round that can be effective on medium-size game at shorter range; cartridges cost about 90¢ each. Twenty-gauge shot-shells can cost as little as $5 per box of 25.)

The single-shot, break-open-action **Harrington & Richardson Topper Junior** is an inexpensive starter shotgun that has been a fixture in American shooting for generations. Cocking it requires pulling the exposed hammer back manu-ally, and a safety mechanism blocks the hammer from reaching the firing pin accidentally. With its wooden stock and a recoil pad, a 22-inch barrel and 12½-inch length of pull, the gun weighs between 5 and 6 pounds. It is available either in .410 bore or 20 gauge. Depending on the finish, MSRP is about $150.

With special adapters (like these **GaugeMates**) it's possible to shoot smaller-gauge cartridges, such as .410s or 28s, in larger-gauge break-action guns, for less recoil. However, 12- and 20-gauge cartridges cost as little as $5 per box of 25, while .410 or 28-gauge ammunition may be twice as much.

Steve Helsley

Mossberg's Model 505 Youth pump-action repeating shotgun, with its 20-inch, ventilated-rib barrel, hardwood stock and a 12-inch length of pull, is a nicely scaled-down version of one of the company's most popular adult guns. The four-shot magazine tube comes with a plug that can convert the gun to single-shot operation. The 20-gauge version has interchangeable choke tubes; the .410 model has a fixed-choke barrel. Weight is 5¼ pounds; MSRP is $389.

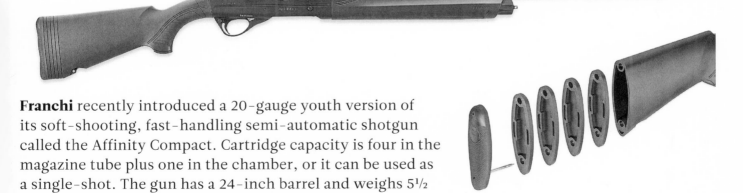

Franchi recently introduced a 20-gauge youth version of its soft-shooting, fast-handling semi-automatic shotgun called the Affinity Compact. Cartridge capacity is four in the magazine tube plus one in the chamber, or it can be used as a single-shot. The gun has a 24-inch barrel and weighs 5½ pounds. The length of pull is 12⅜ inches but, with spacers that can be added to the buttstock, as shown, this can grow in quarter-inch increments to 13⅜ inches as the shooter matures. Also included are shims to change the angle of the stock, for different physiques, and two screw-in choke tubes. MSRP is $899 in black, $999 in camo.

One of the most popular centerfire rifles for young shooters is the **Tikka T3** bolt-action chambered for the light-recoiling, relatively inexpensive (25¢ per round) .223 Remington cartridge. The T3 is available in more than a dozen configurations, all superbly accurate, including left-handed versions. This Lite model with a synthetic stock, a 20-inch barrel and a detachable four-round box magazine weighs less than 6 pounds. MSRP is $625 without a scope or other sights.

Another good first centerfire rifle for younger shooters (who have learned to handle a semi-automatic) is the light, compact **M1 carbine**. It fires a .30-caliber cartridge developed for the US Army in WWII, recoil is minimal and ammunition can cost as little as 50¢ per round in quantity. New M1s are made by Auto-Ordnance (MSRP is $815), but there are many thousands of these rifles on the secondhand or surplus market.

Passive Shooting Safety

Protection for Eyes, Ears and Other Body Parts

Every shooter, no matter how safe and skillful he or she is in handling guns, has to protect himself or herself from two kinds of incidental injury. Damage to hearing can result every time he or she fires a gun or is near someone who does; and the eyes are also at risk any time shots are fired. Fortunately, defending against both injuries is easy and inexpensive.

HEARING PROTECTION

Many shooters, particularly those who've been at it for decades, suffer some degree of hearing impairment. Many also have tinnitus, a high-pitched buzzing in one or both ears. Some audio loss can be compensated for electronically, but tinnitus can't be cured and never goes away.

Both problems can easily be prevented by wearing hearing protection when shooting. The goal is to keep the sonic blast of a too-loud sound wave from reaching the sensitive micro-hairs inside the ear. A single shot (or any too-loud noise) can cause damage, and the ear can't heal itself or be repaired.

The louder the noise, the worse the damage. Air guns generally don't make enough noise to be harmful. A .22 makes a sharp *crack!*—not a tremendous noise, but over time the effect adds up. Our ears don't "rest" in between shooting sessions and then start fresh again.

Experienced shooters wear plugs in their ears or muffs over

What the well-dressed competition pistol shooter wears: Shatter-resistant glasses, hearing protection (probably with soft foam in-the-ear plugs beneath the muffs) and a cap. Note the empty shell being ejected from the gun.

A .22 round does not make a tremendous bang, but over time the effect adds up. Ears don't "rest" in between shooting sessions and then start fresh again. Hearing protection is always needed, and in this case it must fit a smaller head.

their ears. At least for target shooting, we recommend using both together. This doesn't interfere with shooting; the reduction in noise actually improves most shooters' accuracy and (in high-powered guns) even seems to reduce the perception of recoil.

Target shooters have no excuse for not wearing hearing protection. Hunters, on the other hand, must hear every little sound that occurs around them. Some hunters rationalize that, since they don't shoot often, they can get by with naked ears. It's true that a deer hunter might fire only one or two rounds in an entire season, but a single blast can cause loss, and the loss is cumulative.

The best solution for hunters is very expensive: electronic plugs that allow normal sounds to enter the ear but instantly shut down when they detect a noise that's too loud. (Some even amplify ambient sounds.) These must be custom-fitted, so a youngster might need several pairs before his or her ears stop growing.

The next best thing is very *in*expensive: soft foam plugs that expand to fill the ear canal and block the worst of a gunshot. Some hunters put these plugs halfway into their ears so they can hear, and then push them all the way in when it's time to shoot—if they remember and if they have the chance.

Some over-the-ear muffs have electronic sound enhancement built in, but earmuffs can be too cumbersome or hot for hunting.

Everyone, not just shooters, is exposed to noises that are too loud. If you can hear the music your kids are listening to in their earbuds, it's too loud; they don't notice it yet, but they're losing acuity and lowering the threshold for more damage. Leaf blowers, lawn mowers and chainsaws will do damage, as will music at most dance clubs and rock concerts, certain motorcycles and just about every airplane engine. These noises are likely not as momentarily loud as a gunshot, but they go on for much longer.

If your youngster mows the lawn or uses a snowblower, he or she should probably wear the same ear protection he or she uses for shooting.

VISION PROTECTION

Losing some hearing is bad enough, but an eye? It doesn't take much to injure or destroy an eye; even worse, something striking the eye could penetrate the back of the eye socket and enter the brain.

For shooters, hearing damage is certain unless they protect their ears; eye injuries result from bad judgment or bad luck. BBs, pellets, bullets and fragments thereof can ricochet back at a shooter. Some guns eject empty cartridge cases with considerable force. Sharp pieces fly off in every direction when clay pigeons are hit. Hunters dodge twigs and brush. In worst-case scenarios, guns can explode and fling shrapnel around or simply let hot combustion gasses escape. We won't even mention paintballs.

Proper shooting glasses stand between vulnerable eyes and all of these things. Don't rely on ordinary sunglasses or eyeglasses to stop a shotgun pellet or a bit of shrapnel. They may stop it,

More expensive shooting glasses, such as these Rangers, offer interchangeable lenses in a dozen or more colors and come in different frame widths.

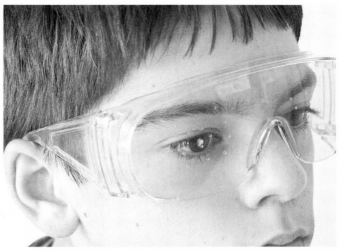

Steve Helsley

Effective shooting glasses for youngsters don't have to be expensive. This type has protective side panels, and the large frame fits over some eyeglasses. If the shooter also wears hearing-protection muffs, make sure the temple bars of the glasses don't break the soundproofing seal around the ear.

but if they shatter, the eye receives not only the pellet but also shards of broken lens.

Impact-resistant glass is heavy. The best shooting lenses are made of special tough plastics: CR-39, polycarbonates or Trivex. CR-39 dates back to WWII and is very tough and durable and about half the weight of glass. Polycarbonates (such as Lexan) came along in the 1970s for aircraft windshields and helmet visors. Trivex is just as strong but thinner and lighter and has better optical qualities. The latter two materials also block ultraviolet light, but they are softer than CR-39 and need scratch-resistant coatings.

If your youngster wears eyeglasses, you can find shooting glasses that fit over them. Wraparound lenses offer more side protection, but the extra curvature of the lenses may cause some distortion. Some shooting glasses have thick temples (earpieces) that ruin the seal of protective earmuffs.

More-expensive shooting glasses come with interchangeable lenses. Shooters who want better visual contrast, to make targets stand out against the sky, use yellow, orange or reddish lenses. Hunters usually want no shift in how they see colors, so they choose neutral gray lenses that reduce sunlight evenly, not just part of it. (Sunglasses, in other words, but impact-resistant ones.) On an overcast day gray lenses may be too dark; in that case shift to clear ones. It's important to make sure that lenses are mounted properly in the frames, so they don't come out just when they're needed most.

HATS, GLOVES, RECOIL PADS

Thin, close-fitting gloves give decent trigger feel and shouldn't interfere with handling cartridges when reloading. They protect the hands somewhat from a hot gun barrel when doing a lot of shooting. On a cold day they're warm and on a hot day they soak up some sweat, and in both cases they can improve one's grip on a gun. High-quality shooting gloves are expensive, though, and kids tend to outgrow clothing quickly.

To go with shooting glasses, an ordinary ball cap helps protect the head and face from

Snug-fitting, sensitive shooting gloves can be very useful, but not necessarily for kids who are just plinking with single-shot .22 rifles.

flying debris as well as keeps the sun out of a shooter's eyes.

Shooting shirts and jackets with patches on the shoulders don't absorb much recoil—which won't be a problem anyway if your youngster is shooting a .22. The real value of those garments is that they help a shooter (especially a shotgun shooter) bring the gun to his shoulder quickly

without snagging buttons, snaps or seams along the way. They generally aren't available in young sizes, however.

Some companies offer foam or gel recoil pads that strap onto the shoulder or fit into a pocket on a shirt. These can soak up some kick. If your youngster's mentor has one, it could be useful in helping get used to a new, harder-recoiling gun.

This is a foam-filled recoil pad that straps on over a shirt or light jacket. Generally, a soft pad on the butt of the gun is more useful, but not all guns have them.

Shooting Safely

What Your Youngster Has to Learn About Gun Safety

Since about 1950, shooting has become such an extraordinarily accident-free pastime because two generations of Americans have had gun-safety rules and etiquette drummed into them—backed up by the efforts of organizations, manufacturers and even legislators. If driver education were taught so comprehensively, automobile accidents would all but disappear.

If you've only scanned the Table of Contents of *The Gun Book for Boys*, you know that we, too, have devoted considerable ink to the subject. However, all we can do is influence; we have no control over how your novice handles guns, or ammunition, or himself or herself while shooting. Furthermore, unless you're with your youngster every minute while he or she is so engaged, you can't exert any direct control either.

Your youngster's mentor; coaches or instructors, if any; and friends with whom he or she shares an interest in guns all have significant influence over his or her development as a safe shooter. Fortunately, unless they arrived recently from some other planet, they too were brought up in the same culture of active gun safety.

For your own edification, here are the rules as laid down in *The Gun Book for Boys*. Virtually every shooter in America will recognize them. We have had them drummed into us since very early days; now we're paying them forward.

THE 15 COMMANDMENTS OF GUN SAFETY

1. Always assume that a gun is loaded, and treat it accordingly.

2. Every time a gun is handled for any reason, check to see that it is unloaded. Always open a gun's action when you pass it to someone else. Always open a gun's action when shooting is done.

3. Keep the gun pointed in the safest-possible direction, and always be aware of where it's pointing. A safe direction is one where an accidental discharge of the gun will not cause injury or damage.

4. Don't point a gun at anything you're not willing to destroy.

5. Always keep your finger off the trigger and outside the trigger guard until you're ready to shoot.

6. Keep the safety catch on until you're ready to shoot.

7. Be sure your target is what you want to shoot. Never shoot at a target that is only a movement, color, sound or unidentifiable shape. Be aware of your surroundings before you shoot.

8. Always remember that if the bullet misses or passes through the target, it could hit something or someone behind it.

9. If in doubt, **DON'T SHOOT**.

10. Use only the proper ammunition.

11. Keep the gun unloaded until you are ready to use it.

12. Don't rely on the gun's safety catch to prevent it from firing.

13. Keep the barrel clear of obstructions and the gun clean and functioning.

14. Be completely familiar with your gun and know how to operate it, including how to load and unload it and clear a malfunction. Many guns are different; never assume that what applies to one make or model is the same on another.

15. When the gun is not in your hands, safety is still important. Store your gun safely and securely. Put an approved safety device, such as a trigger lock or cable lock, on the gun so it can't be fired. Store the ammunition somewhere else that is equally safe and secure.

As comprehensive as this list is, it still has to be backed up by understanding. *The Gun Book for Boys* expands on exactly what constitutes "proper ammunition" (No. 10, above), why a safety catch is important (No. 6) even if it isn't foolproof (No. 12), and why layers of good safety habits can protect against both a true accident and just a momentary lapse.

Understanding and then repetition convert rules into unbreakable habits.

THE BIRD HUNTER'S BLUE SKY RULE

Since gamebirds fly unpredictably, shotguns can easily wind up pointed in unsafe directions—toward another hunter, for example, or at a dog. Muzzle control (Commandment No. 3) is one of the absolute, no-exceptions rules. For hunters caught up in the excitement of a bird's flush, muzzle control means the Blue Sky Rule: Don't shoot at a bird unless you can see sky around it. That means the bird is high enough in the air that the shot won't hit anyone on the ground.

An accidental discharge is just a scary moment if the gun is pointed in a harmless direction when it happens.

Left: "It's OK, I've got another foot." This shows very poor muzzle safety, and the shotgun's action is closed too! What if the gun is loaded?

Right: Where is the rifle pointing? And this bolt is closed too.

Steve Helsley

Steve Helsley

Steve Helsley

More bad muzzle control. What's in the line of fire? This over/under shotgun should be pointed at the ground—and its action should be open.

One reason many bird hunters like double guns is that the actions can be opened, which lets everyone around know that the gun is completely safe, even with cartridges still in the chambers.

THE CARDINAL RULES OF GUN SAFETY

*I*f you go to the range with your shooter and his or her mentor once in a while—and you should, for many reasons—you'll be able to assess your child's safety habits and skills for yourself. You can do this at home as well. Watch your youngster as he retrieves his gun from storage, slips it into the case and carries it to the car, and then again when he returns, unpacks it, checks it, cleans it and puts it back into the safe.

If you can't remember all 15 Commandments, there are four cardinal rules that are essential to safety:

1. Always assume a gun is loaded.

2. Never load a gun until it is time to use it.

3. Never point a gun at anything you don't wish to destroy.

4. Keep your finger off the trigger until you are ready to destroy your target.

If now you go back and re-read "Firearms Courtesy" in "Gun Basics," you'll see that those rules of etiquette are grounded in large part on safety rules.

Silvio Calabi

Slung over the shoulder with the muzzle up is a safe way to carry a rifle while hunting.

Storing Guns & Ammunition

Proper Storage Is an Important Part of Gun Safety

When guns are not being used—which, after all, is most of the time—they have to be kept where "unauthorized users" can't get at them. The same thing goes for ammunition.

If you live in an urban or suburban area, there may be a shooting club or range that offers gun storage on site (and a well-thought-out storage policy), as there are in Britain and Europe. If a gun never comes home, home storage isn't a concern.

An "unauthorized user" in this case is not only a brother, sister, other relative or friend of your young shooter (or an intruder), it's also the shooter himself or herself. Until your youngster has proven to be a responsible shooter, you should control access to guns.

Guns should be kept in a vault or safe specially built for the purpose with some sort of key or combination lock on the door. Safes come in all sizes for as few as a half-dozen long guns to 30 or more. Some are made of sheet metal and are relatively light; these should be lagged to the floor or a wall. True gun safes may weigh hundreds of pounds, so no one can walk off with them easily, and they may be humidity-controlled or fire-resistant. Such a safe is gilding

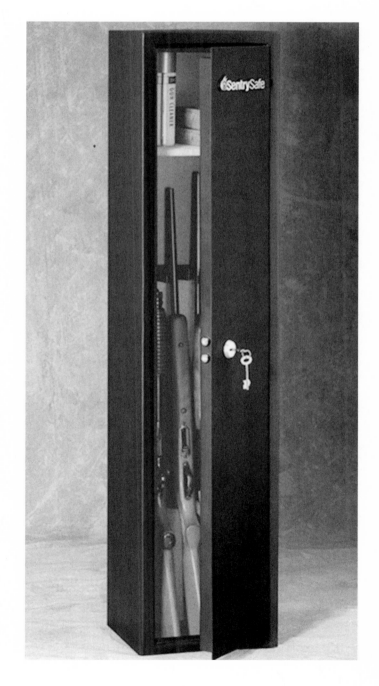

Gun vaults come in all sizes, for as few as a half-dozen long guns to 30 or more. This is an inexpensive, relatively light-weight Sentry-brand steel locker that should be fastened to the floor or a wall.

A pistol with a combination-type trigger lock. The National Shooting Sports Foundation provides free safety kits that include a gun lock.

the lily for a BB gun and a couple of .22s, but if your family has other personal posses- sions that should be stored se- curely—jewelry, documents, gold coins—this might be a good time for such an invest- ment.

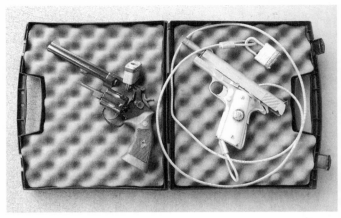

Ordinary household locks can keep guns from being used by the wrong people. The revolver has a padlock around its top strap. The pistol has a bicycle cable threaded through its slide and grip that can also be looped around something unmov- able like a beam or a post.

In any case, put the safe out of sight in a closet, or camouflage it as furniture to deflect cu- rious eyes. A throw and a pillow top can make a horizontal gun chest look like a bench seat or the footboard of a bed.

• Merely hiding a gun or ammunition in a closet is no substitute for locked storage. Kids are natu- ral snoops and can find about anything.

• When a gun is not in use, it should be cleaned promptly and put away. Gun-cleaning instruc- tions (and information about gun safes) are pro- vided in *The Gun Book for Boys*. It should hardly need saying, but your youngster's guns must be stored unloaded.

A caution: Using a gun doesn't necessarily mean

shooting it. The chapter called "Target Practice" in the boys' book recommends several useful gun-handling exercises that are safe to do in- doors without ammunition.

• Another reason for storing guns securely is to keep them clean and protected from moisture and even damage by insects or rodents. Guns stored in cases (in a vault) should be wiped down with a rust-preventive (light oil or silicon) and checked periodically.

◆━━◆◆◆━━◆

LEGAL STORAGE REQUIREMENTS

*I*f a gun is stored "negligently"—which could be in an unlocked place, or a closet, or a wooden drawer or cabinet that could be broken into, or without disabling it with a trigger lock or something similar—and an unauthorized user causes harm with it, you may be charged with a crime. It's important to be in compliance with state or municipal laws.

Some municipalities require gun owners to put locks on the triggers or somehow block the

actions when they put their guns away. Such locks are inexpensive and easy to find; more and more manufacturers and retailers are including them with every gun they sell. The National Shooting Sports Foundation provides free safety kits that include a gun lock. These are distributed through police departments. Go to www.projectchildsafe. org to see if they're available in your area.

So-called takedown guns can easily be disas- sembled into two sections (barrel and stock). This

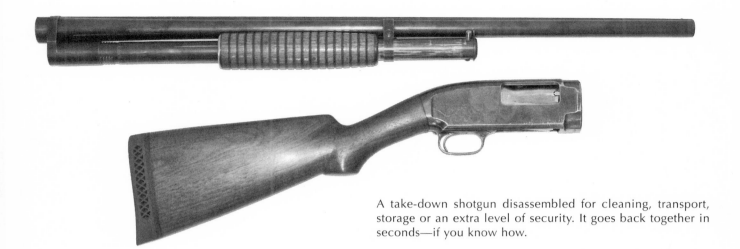

A take-down shotgun disassembled for cleaning, transport, storage or an extra level of security. It goes back together in seconds—if you know how.

is convenient for traveling and it makes cleaning the gun easier, but it also provides an extra layer of security if the gun is stored taken apart. The potential for accidental shootings goes way down if someone has to a) get at the gun, b) unpack it and put it together or pry off the trigger lock, and then c) find the ammunition and load it.

WHAT ABOUT AMMUNITION?

Many adult shooters store ammunition in the same vault or safe with their guns, but securing the ammunition under lock and key somewhere else will provide you with another degree of control over your youngster's shooting. A few boxes of .22 cartridges should fit in the file drawer where you lock up family documents. Shotgun ammunition takes up more space; you might buy two boxes (usually 50 rounds) at a time when your youngster goes out to shoot clay pigeons and use them all up.

Although it's filled with gunpowder, modern ammunition is very stable. Even in a raging house fire, ammunition won't explode; it simply pops off. The combustion has to be contained in a tight space, such as a gun barrel, for enough pressure to build up to launch a bullet. Ammunition is also generally water-resistant and doesn't corrode easily.

You must decide with your young shooter how to control his or her access to guns and ammunition. This involves a wide range of factors, including where you live, what sort of a gun your youngster has and where he or she shoots it, and your child's maturity and level of responsibility. The simplest approach is to keep the key(s) and/or combination(s) to the gun vault and ammunition storage to yourself and require your youngster to come to you for access. Then you can ask the important who, what, when and where questions.

Precautions such as these have driven accidental shootings to historically low levels in the US.

Transporting Guns

What's Safe & Legal Depends Partly on Where You Are—and Where You're Going

Unless you live on a farm or ranch or you have an indoor shooting range at home (or your youngster stores his or her gun at a range), chances are that you or your child's mentor will have to transport your youngster and a gun to someplace where he or she can shoot. Naturally, there are federal, state and possibly local laws to be aware of, plus some common-sense guidelines.

What follows is necessarily general because state and local laws vary and all laws may change. You must know the rules for where you live. The information is available on Websites created by state fish and game departments, towns and cities, and police departments. (Go back to "Familiarize Yourself with Firearms Laws" in "Junior Wants to Shoot! Now What?")

In general, you may transport a gun and ammunition by car if the gun is unloaded and locked in the trunk in a case. No trunk? Then the gun should be in some other locked container outside the passenger compartment, like a toolbox in a pickup-truck bed or a camper trailer.

Licensed hunters can usually carry their guns in the passenger compartment of a car—but often not at night, since hunting game after dark is illegal. Carrying guns in boats, ATVs or snow machines may be regulated too.

Traveling with guns on commercial airliners, trains, buses and ships is strictly controlled. Some of these carriers allow passengers to transport guns, some do not; all you can do is inquire. Most airlines do transport guns. (They must be in

A soft case, like this one from Boyt for a takedown gun, is excellent protection against bumps and scratches, but it meets no legal security requirements.

Silvio Calabi

a locked, hard-sided case, declared on check-in, and then carried as baggage in the storage hold of the plane. Ammunition also has to be declared, checked, and then stowed in the hold, but it can go in ordinary luggage. There are also limits to the amount of ammunition you can transport.) Shipping and receiving guns and ammunition by mail or parcel post is regulated too, both by federal law and the carriers themselves.

National parks, military bases and properties that belong to the federal government usually have their own firearms rules.

This probably isn't relevant to your youngster, but just so you know: Wearing a loaded handgun openly in a holster is legal in some places and not in others. Some states require a permit to carry concealed firearms; a few do not.

Taking your son or daughter to a local range or (in a rural area) gravel pit or open field to shoot is usually very simple—at least once the necessary permits, if any, are obtained. Things can get complicated, however, if you wish to drive from one state to another with firearms. Even within federal laws, what is perfectly legal in, say, Vermont may call for a mandatory prison stay in Massachusetts. If

your youngster wants to bring a BB gun on the family's annual RV holiday, find a copy of the latest edition of the *Traveler's Guide to the Firearm Laws of the Fifty States*, by J. Scott Kappas, attorney at law. It's widely available everywhere from gun stores to Amazon.com.

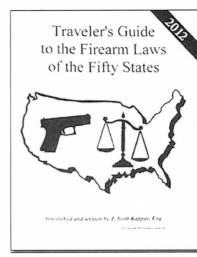

Author and attorney J. Scott Kappas frequently updates his *Traveler's Guide* to stay abreast of changes in state gun laws.

SAFETY AND COMMON SENSE

Even if you live in an area where a gun rack in the back window of a pickup truck is still a common sight, it's best to put a gun in a case (hard or soft) when it's time to transport it somewhere. If the gun has a trigger lock or some other safety device on it, leave it in place. Naturally, the gun should be unloaded too. A carrying case protects a gun from scrapes and dirt and also hides it. Even if it's legal to leave a gun in view—inside a locked car, for example—it may motivate some people to call the police. Also, leaving a gun in plain sight can encourage a thief

An inexpensive, foam-lined, plastic-sided case from Plano. This can be a good way to transport a gun in the trunk of a car, but it won't stand up to the rigors of air travel.

to break in and grab it. Stow cased guns and their ammunition in the trunk, and lock it.

BRINGING GUNS TO SCHOOL

Never, under any circumstances. The federal Gun-Free School Zones Act of 1990 and 1996 prohibits firearms on and within 1,000 feet of any private or public school property, kindergarten through 12th grade, except in the possession of a police officer, a licensed school security guard or someone else who is authorized by the state to carry a gun.

The federal law applies to firearms, but state or local laws may add BB and pellet guns, Airsoft and Paintball guns, and even toy guns.

If your son is old enough to drive to school, and it's hunting season and he's planning to go sit in a duck blind that afternoon—he will be in violation of the law even if his gun is in a locked case in the locked trunk of the car in the school parking lot. He must go home after classes and get his gun and gear, and then go hunting.

A few schools have organized, supervised shooting teams, usually for smallbore-rifle or for some type of shotgunning competition. These schools have plenty of rules and regulations covering every aspect of this, and the guns aren't kept at the school.

Travel with a (legal) firearm and ammunition is regulated at both ends of the trip. Transporting a gun by commercial airline is permitted if the gun is unloaded and locked in a tough, hard-sided case such as this one made of aluminum. The gun must be declared at the airport. A Transportation Security Administration officer will open the case to inspect the gun and, if applicable, check its serial number against a Customs form or a gun permit. On approval, the case is re-locked and stowed in the baggage hold of the plane. Upon arrival, the gun is usually hand-delivered by a security officer to the traveler. Ammunition comes under separate restrictions imposed by TSA, the airline and sometimes the destination.

Silvio Calabi

Bringing History to Life

If Only Guns Could Talk

More than 50 years ago, at breakfast on one of the authors' 14th birthday, his mother presented him with a battered WWII Japanese army rifle. She announced that it had been bought—for $2—from an antique dealer who "didn't like guns." The overjoyed and slightly stunned boy could tell it was a military rifle, but that was the extent of his knowledge. Shortly followed a visit to a local gunshop for a $5 box of cartridges, and then a trip to a shooting range.

(Why a beat-up gun as a birthday present? "She knew I liked to shoot—a .22 and a couple of BB guns—so she just assumed I'd like it. And for $2 she thought she couldn't go wrong. I've still got it.")

From then on, whenever the boy could scrape together $10 or $15, he would go to the gunshop, escorted by Mom or Dad, to browse the racks and add another foreign (British, Russian, French, whatever) military rifle to his collection. (The shop is still in business, probably still inspiring daydreams among 14-year-olds.) He didn't necessarily know where the countries of origin were or what conflicts the rifles might have served in; like most kids, he thought history was boring.

That changed the following Christmas, when the boy unwrapped a copy of *Small Arms of the World,* by Walter H.B. Smith. This book was first published in 1943 as a basic reference for military personnel. In 723 pages and thousands of illustrations, Smith put the various war-surplus rifles into historical context: *Did the Enfield come ashore at Gallipoli in the hands of a New Zealand trooper? Was the Mosin-Nagant dragged through the mud and snow of Stalingrad? Had the birthday rifle been pried from the cold hands of an Imperial Japanese soldier who committed hara-kiri at Iwo Jima?* The notion that those scruffy, bruised relics might have taken part in momentous events in distant and exotic places triggered (oh, yes) an

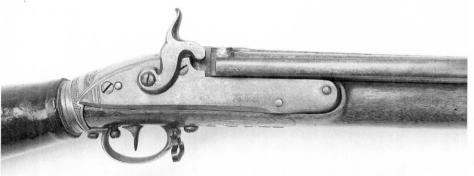

National Firearms Museum

An Italian Girandoni air rifle like this one was Lewis and Clark's "secret weapon" on their expedition across the wilderness from 1804 to 1806. Whenever their Corps of Discovery met an Indian band, Lewis and Clark and their officers dressed up in their uniforms and put on a shooting demonstration—with the Girandoni. It seems the Indians were always impressed with this powerful, accurate and unusually rapid-firing weapon. Perhaps assuming that each of the Whites had one of these deadly rifles, they let the party continue. Had the expedition been wiped out and the Indians seized its powder and shot, pistols, rifles, muskets, shotguns, blunderbusses and one swivel cannon, American and possibly even European history could have developed very differently.

Steve Helsley Collection

An ad from the April 1962 issue of *American Rifleman* magazine. The US market was then awash with war-surplus material at giveaway prices. One importer offered German 37mm anti-tank guns ("the pride of Rommel's Afrika Corps") for $300. Each cannon was mounted on wheels and was 12 feet long and weighed 700 pounds, so shipping was $25 extra. Ammunition cost $1.50 per round.

undiminished passion for history. The book became the first volume in what is now a significant library.

Today *Small Arms of the World* is in its 12th edition, and it is part of the "further reading" we recommend in *The Gun Book for Boys.*

For better or worse, since the 13th Century firearms have been at the center of history. Leonardo da Vinci designed them, Meriwether Lewis and Richard Clark used them to protect and feed their Corps of Discovery as they explored the American West, and with one shot Gavrilo Princip set in motion the events that led to World War I. Oh, and the American Revolution was sparked by an attempt to confiscate colonists' guns.

Just a glance at the bibliography of *The Gun Book for Boys* will indicate the historical sweep covered by that book. One reference—*The Gun*, by C.J. Chivers—is the story of the AK-47, a rifle that may have had a greater impact on the 20th Century than the atomic bomb. Today our military opponents are armed with AKs and, in those places that consider America the "great Satan," newborn boys are named Kalash in honor of M.T. Kalashnikov, the inventor of the AK-47. Sobering stuff, and worth knowing.

Serious gun collectors are almost invariably interested in

history. We hope that if you decide it's appropriate for your child to learn the safe, responsible use of firearms, you will also steer that enthu-

siasm into a grasp of the historical and cultural aspects of the guns that interest them.

Dueling pistols, such as this pair made by William & John Rigby in Dublin in 1828, were often historically significant—depending on which prominent citizens used them. The most famous duel in American history took place on July 11, 1804, in New Jersey, when Col. Aaron Burr fatally wounded Gen. Alexander Hamilton. Burr was then Vice-President of the United States and later started the company that became the Chase Manhattan Bank; Hamilton had been the first Secretary of the US Treasury.

Guns as Introductions to Tools

Gun-Fiddling Can Enable All Manner of Household & Garden Projects

*I*t's been our general observation that, just as boys are drawn to guns more than girls are, many of the males of our species also enjoy using tools. But it's becoming a lost art. Once upon a time, a rite of passage for a teenage American male was working on his third-hand car—rebuilding the carburetor, replacing the generator with one scavenged from the junkyard, pounding out dents. This involved learning to use hand tools, a process that was aided by high-school shop classes. Some kids also applied what we learned in shop to firearms repair and restoration.

One of the authors brought his war-surplus .45 Webley revolver to Mr. Normandin's high-school metal shop to make some modifications for class credit. It never occurred to the author, Mr. Normandin or, apparently, anyone else that doing so might create an "issue." (Issues were called "problems" back then.) There was precedent, though: Several years earlier, with Mom's help, the boy had brought his great-great-grandfather's Civil War musket to Mr. Fishburn's sixth-grade class for show & tell.

Equally startling, in hindsight, was that the high school had a rifle range, and students in the Junior ROTC program carried their cased .22 rifles on campus. Egad! How did anyone survive?

This was not Rattlesnake Hollow, Montana, either; it was the Los Angeles Unified School District, where officials had weightier issues to deal with: provocative dance gyrations, loud exhaust pipes, ducktail haircuts and rock & roll lyrics! No

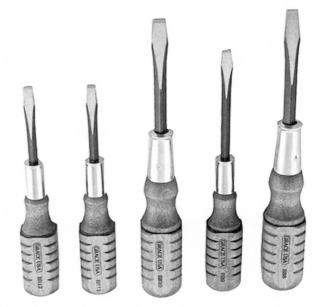

These hardened tool-steel screwdrivers ("turnscrews" in Britain) from Brownell's Supply have square shanks, hand-filling hardwood handles and nickel-silver ferrules, and they are hollow-ground. A hollow-ground screwdriver has a tip with parallel sides that is shaped to fill the slot exactly, in order to apply even pressure without marring the head of the screw. (And you thought they were for prying open cans of paint.)

one got their knickers in a knot over an old gun or a target rifle.

Fast-forward to today. High-school shop classes have been replaced by vo-tech schools where "those other kids" go. Messing about with cars is a memory, and kids now cope with a flat tire by texting AAA on their smartphones. Even your authors gave up auto repair decades ago, when electronic fuel injection replaced carburetors. But the mechanical skills we learned from working on cars and guns have stayed with us.

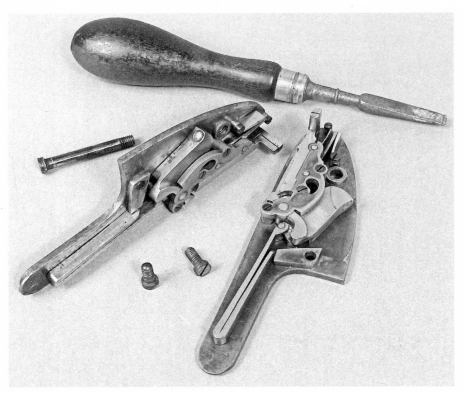

Simply removing (and then replacing) the locks from a double-barreled gun, to check for wear and lubrication, requires some know-how, dexterity and the proper tool—in this case a screwdriver with a blade fitted exactly to the slit in the screw heads.

a sow's ear into some semblance of a silk purse. We were proud of our "restorations," although we cringe a bit now in light of what we've learned since then.

Slowly the quality of work improved, along with the complexity of the projects. Later came drill presses and lathes, spring tempering and welding. Gun-fiddling in turn enabled all manner of household and garden projects, from tuning up the lawn mower to furniture restoration, and it became useful on those Christmases when boxes that announced "some assembly required" were unwrapped.

One of the themes in *The Gun Book for Boys* is "find a pastime that will last a lifetime." The shooting sports can involve high-level competition, hunting, camping, conservation and global travel. Simply tinkering with guns fosters the self-confidence and creativity that derives from skills with tools. Can you take apart and diagnose a bum wall thermostat? Refinish a deck chair? Change the SIM card in your phone? Do you wish your teenager knew how to do such things? Guns and shooting may just be more useful in the long run than Facebook or playing Office Zombie online.

Imagine an old shotgun found in a barn, an unpleasant mix of rust, dents and oil-soaked wood with some parts broken and others missing. Fascinating! This was our introduction to wood and metalwork, as well as disassembly of a fairly complex mechanism (followed, one hoped, by successful reassembly, with a minimum of parts left over). It took files, solvents, sandpaper and steel wool, screwdrivers, punches and more, as well as time, study and ingenuity to turn such

Shooting as a Family Activity

First, It's Great Fun

Many years ago, at the beginning of the political debate about what came to be called assault weapons (see "Meet the AR-15," in "Choosing a First Gun"), one of the authors found himself involved. His boss, a state attorney general, was in favor of a bill to ban assault weapons. Senior staff members for the state senator who was behind the bill asked to be briefed on the difference between fully automatic weapons (such as machine guns, submachine guns and assault rifles) and semi-automatic firearms. They didn't know a shotgun from a slingshot, so the AG's office arranged a hands-on demonstration at a shooting range. One of the demo arms was a 9mm Heckler & Koch MP5. It is to submachine guns what the Ruger 10/22 is to .22 rifles—the gold standard. With negligible recoil, compact dimensions and light weight, it is user-friendly for veterans and newbies alike.

The senator's ranking staffer was a woman who made no secret of her dislike for guns. After the appropriate coaching, with ear and eye protection in place, she was handed the MP5 with a 30-round magazine. Firing a few single rounds at the target diminished her anxiety to where the selective-fire switch could be flipped, and she graduated to repeated two- and three-shot bursts. Then it was rock & roll time: With a fresh magazine, she let it rip—*brrrrraap!* Empty brass cases were flying everywhere.

At this point most new shooters laugh in sheer disbelief and delight. She managed to restrain herself to a huge grin, and then she sheepishly asked, "May I do it again?"

As full-auto shooters like to say, "Happiness is a warm machine gun!"

Machine guns represent a tiny segment of the shooting-sports world. They are heavily regulated (not banned, as most people think), and they're expensive to buy and to "feed." But they're great fun.

Shooting any kind of gun is fun. There is something uniquely gratifying about hitting a target with a gun, especially if the target breaks (or falls over, or whirls around or, better yet, explodes). Gunfire itself—the noise and recoil, even the smell of burned powder—gets us stirred up. Just like fireworks.

TARGET SHOOTING

Shooting is a skill, and humans are hard-wired to appreciate and reward skill—in this case accuracy. Skills are to be developed, which requires proper equipment and practice, and then tested.

A shooting range can be a fine place for family fun on a weekend, with a snack bar or picnic tables and perhaps a pro shop that sells ammunition, ear plugs, targets and other supplies. For safety, range officers monitor the shooting activities.

Visit any range and you'll see shooters sitting at tables with their rifles or handguns propped up on sandbags or some other kind of rest, carefully squeezing off rounds at targets anywhere from 25 to 500 yards distant. They may be testing ammunition they've reloaded, to find the most accurate combinations of powder, primer and bullet. They may be adjusting the sights on their guns before hunting season. They

may just be working on their skills. Repeatedly hitting a tiny bull's-eye at long range takes not only good equipment but also discipline: visual concentration, steady hands, a gentle trigger squeeze, even proper breathing control.

Many rifle and handgun shooters don't hunt and will never participate in formal competition; instead they gather with like-minded friends or relatives and shoot holes in paper, and then go have coffee.

Shotgun shooting also can be an informal weekend pastime. These youngsters are having fun shooting trap under the supervision of the scorekeeper (and spectators) behind them.

Shotgunners gather at trap, skeet or sporting clays fields (see "Competition" in *The Gun Book for Boys*) on a Saturday for their version of the same thing: They bang away at clay pigeons zooming off at all angles and speeds. This is as different from shooting at paper targets as ice-skating is from jogging, and newcomers often think it's much more fun than punching holes in static targets. There's an almost balletic grace to it, and shattering a flying claybird into a puff of dust is tremendously satisfying.

Like rifle and handgun shooters, most shotgunners don't compete in anything more rigorous than the occasional club championship.

COMPETITIVE SHOOTING

*W*hen it comes to formal competition with shotguns, rifles and handguns, things can get serious quickly. Famous trophies, Olympic medals, big cash prizes and even college scholarships may be on the line. (*The Gun Book for Boys* explores this in considerable depth.) Official matches are closely regulated by sanctioning bodies. The types of guns, calibers, ammunition, sights, distances and targets are standardized. Certain matches are steeped in tradition too. The Leech Cup, for example, was first contested in 1874 by the Irish and American national teams shooting at 1,000 yards—more than a half-mile. It still takes place today.

For those who shun "normal" targets and competition, there are almost unlimited options. Want to shoot infantry rifles at 1,000 yards? Air pistols at 10 meters? Blackpowder rifles at silhouettes of game animals? The guns of the Wild West? Submachine guns? BB guns? Sniper rifles? Rimfire .22s while skiing cross-country (aka biathlon)?

Wingshooting can become high-pressure competition too. Armed with a custom-fitted and specially equipped shotgun, US Army Marksmanship Unit member Spc. Walton Glenn Eller III takes a gold medal with an Olympic record score of 190 in doubles trap at the 2008 Games in Beijing.

Antique shotguns? For all of these and many more, there are organized forms of competition, complete with rules, prizes and sponsors, at every level from local to national to international.

PLINKING

*I*f you've never "plinked," it's not necessarily an easy concept to grasp. It's like shooting hoops, throwing snowballs, skipping stones across a pond, pitching pennies (we're dating ourselves) or many of the other highly informal, semi-competitive fun things that males get up to when left to their own devices. Plinking can

be done with any sort of gun, but a .22 rimfire is usually the choice; ammunition is dirt cheap, and there's little noise and no recoil. Any safe (non-ricocheting) target will do: old golf balls, chunks of wood, plastic milk jugs filled with water . . . and now there are commercially made "reactive" targets specifically for plinking.

These happy lads are set for an afternoon of plinking with their .22s. Note their hearing and eye protection and how they're holding their rifles.

Those black plastic guns (aka "assault weapons") that have "no purpose but killing people" are widely used for plinking—and also in formal match competition and now hunting too. Their cartridges cost more than .22 ammunition and the target is likely to be farther away, but the concept is the same.

Imagine two shooters with 5.56mm AR-type rifles vying to hit a log on a hillside at 300 yards. This is plinking too, just like shooting tin cans off a stump at 20 yards with a single-shot .22.

Many family gatherings—birthdays, 4th of July barbecues, summer picnics—traditionally have, or at least once had, a plinking component. It might be shooting clay pigeons thrown with a hand launcher or powdering Necco wafers with a BB gun. For many people, especially those who don't stick with shooting later in life, these are enduring memories.

It's possible that more ammunition is burned up in plinking than in any other kind of sport shooting. Its informal, relaxed nature is ideal for beginners. Priority No. 1 is to be safe; priority No. 2 is to have fun.

Hunting

A Bonding Exercise Like No Other

Very few Americans take up hunting on their own. To some people it seems obsolete, if not barbaric, while to those who are intrigued by it, hunting can be intimidatingly difficult to get started in, at least without a mentor. So if any generalization can be made about hunters, it's that there's often another one somewhere in the family. Hunting is usually passed down through the generations, and therein lies one of its "secrets": Hunting is a unique opportunity for bonding. It is, or should be, a time to pay full and undivided attention to a son or daughter, niece or nephew, partner or close friend, heightened by the need to impart vital information and to be focused, watchful and safe.

As a bonus, hunting puts us in natural, often beautiful surroundings far from traffic, noise and crowds. And no pastime generates more stories and memories than hunting.

All this means that there is much more to hunting than the harvest, and a hunt can be tremendously successful without killing something.

In the 50 million or so American households that own guns, there are 16-plus million licensed firearms hunters. Just as with guns themselves, as we have become increasingly urbanized, much misinformation has sprung up about hunting. If your young shooter is interested in hunting, keep an open mind and please review the following.

A game animal is one that is hunted, for its meat and/or as a trophy. There is small-game hunting, for rabbits, squirrels, foxes, various birds and so on, and big-game hunting. North America and Europe have huntable populations of elk, moose and bears, but for many hunters "big game" means deer. Some big-game hunters travel to Africa or Asia to

Kermit Roosevelt and his father (with trophy eland skulls) in East Africa. Kermit took a break from his freshman year at Harvard in 1909 to go on safari.

hunt the great variety of wild species there, from antelopes to leopard, lion, buffalo and elephant. An African hunt is a safari, which is Swahili for "journey."

President Theodore Roosevelt was one of the first Americans to go on safari, in 1909 and 1910. He spent 15 months in East Africa collecting animal specimens for the Smithsonian Institution and the American Museum of Natural History, and he reported on his trip in magazines and a popular book, *African Game Trails*.

This was the beginning of the safari business, where sportsmen and women hire certified and licensed Professional Hunters (aka PHs) to guide them. Today hunting guides are available throughout the world, not just in Africa.

Whether in pursuit of squirrels or elephants, guided or alone, hunting demands physical fitness and woodcraft, skill with a gun (or bow), time and patience, and sometimes a certain steadiness under pressure. Cable-TV shows are rarely able to convey the realities of hunting in their 22-minute format. No one would watch (or sponsor) a show that featured hours and days of planning, looking, stalking, waiting and sometimes frustration for every minute of actual shooting.

HUNTING FOR MEAT

All around us life-and-death struggles go on constantly: Spiders trap and eat flies, songbirds pluck spiders from their webs, hawks and house cats hunt songbirds, and so on. Within a few miles of downtown New York, Chicago and Los Angeles, coyotes kill and eat deer—as well as house cats and dogs. This isn't a phenomenon that has retreated to the wilds of Alaska or northern Canada.

The eternal predator-prey relationship means survival, but one of the benefits of civilization is that we no longer need to kill and butcher our own meat, whether wild or farm-raised. As a result, some people have come to see hunting as cruel or unjustified, and some even want it banned. Ironically, most of these people buy meat from a market, wear leather shoes and belts and carry leather handbags, but they don't consider how cattle, pigs and sheep are "processed" for market. They probably don't understand ethical hunting either, or the relationship between hunting and conservation.

Hunters ask, which is more natural: stalking and killing a deer or antelope in its own environment and then butchering it yourself,

Now the work begins. This Colorado elk was hunted for meat; now it has to be gutted and removed from the field.

or buying a steak from cattle that were raised in a pen on chemically enhanced feed and then trucked to a factory to be dispatched and cut up on an assembly line?

Many hunters regard what they do as the most honest form of "shopping" for meat, just as many people grow their own vegetables in a garden. And just as gardeners take care of their fields and plants, hunters watch over their resources in many ways. A local fish-and-game club may maintain a stretch of trout stream or plant food plots for game animals, while at the national level the Pittman-Robertson Federal Aid in Wildlife Restoration Act of 1937 distributes the federal excise tax monies collected on the sale of guns and ammunition (reportedly more than $2 billion to date) among the 50 states for wildlife management.

Hunters were instrumental in creating America's network of national and state parks. Hunters were almost alone in lobbying for wildlife protection and management laws across America. Hunters are considered America's most effective and most active conservationists.

If it's properly managed, hunting also helps keep game populations in balance. In much of the US, four-legged predators such as wolves and mountain lions were wiped out long ago, so prey species such as deer would over-populate even further in the absence of hunting. (Collisions between motor vehicles and deer cause about 19,500 injuries each year in the US.) In wilder ecosystems, where natural predators still play significant roles, hunting is managed for minimal impact overall. Commercial hunting, for some part of a wild animal to sell (ivory or rhino horns, skins, feathers or meat), is generally illegal everywhere.

Many people around the world still hunt to put meat on the table. Few Americans would go hungry without it, though, so it's more accurate to say that many of us make a point of eating what we kill and use this as one of our reasons for hunting.

HUNTING FOR TROPHIES

Trophy hunting has an especially bad reputation among people who believe that Modern Man should no longer kill wild animals, especially for sport. Ideally, trophy hunting means using one's abilities to find and kill the best-possible example of some kind of game animal. Trophy hunting isn't hunting strictly for food, but the meat is seldom wasted. It may be given to a nearby village, eaten by the hunter or camp staff or, in some places, taken to a butcher shop to be sold.

The trophy itself—the horns or antlers, skull or skin—is part of the hunter's reward. Keeping a trophy is as natural as hunting itself, and it is a sign of our respect for the animal. A trophy is also a remembrance of days in the field and the rare experience, awe and excitement of being a natural predator once again. Stalking and killing a potentially dangerous animal—the various buffaloes, big cats, bears, elephant, rhino and a few others that "run both

Jofie Lamprecht Photography

A fine trophy. An old African eland bull, one horn long-ago broken short, that had left its genes behind and was nearing the end of its natural life. The pursuit was long and hard.

ways"—brings with it the extra emotion of sheer survival.

About a trophy lion, Robert Ruark wrote: "He was the handsomest lion I had ever seen, in or out of a zoo, and I was not sorry about the collection of him. Already I was beginning to fall into the African way of thinking: that if you properly respect what you are after, and shoot it cleanly and on the animal's terrain, if you imprison in your mind all the wonder of the day from sky to smell to breeze to flowers—then you have not merely killed an animal. You have lent immortality to a beast . . . This is better than letting him grow a few years older, to be killed or crippled by a son and eaten, still alive, by hyenas. Death is not a dreadful thing in Africa—not if you respect the thing you kill, not if you kill to feed your people or your memory."

Man, however, is not only a natural predator but also a competitor. The larger a set of antlers or the heavier a pair of tusks or the bigger a bearskin, the more we tend to value them. "Mine is bigger than yours"—so I am a better hunter and provider than you. But this isn't necessarily so; outstanding trophies have been taken sometimes within steps of camp. And some trophies can simply be bought. A worthy trophy, however, usually calls for days in the field, with hard work, sweat and sometimes frustration and disappointment before final success.

One of the most famous of the old white hunters of East Africa, Philip Percival, used to say, "If you want to have a nice hunt, leave the tape measure at home." That is, forget sheer size and your name in the record books, and concentrate on the quality of the experience instead: the wonders of scenery and wildlife; being in the bush, with its evenings around the campfire with new and old friends; and finding, tracking, outwitting and at last taking a fine trophy—that is, an impressive old animal that has made its contribution to the gene pool and is nearing the end of its natural life.

It may not make sense at first, but this kind of hunting is also the surest way to protect wild game. In Africa, for example, tribal people who live in the bush generally regard wild animals as a nuisance. Lions and leopards prey on their goats and cattle (and threaten them and their families), while other game, from elephants to warthogs, raid their crops. Given the chance, they kill these animals any way they can, often with traps or poison, even if it's illegal. But if they get a share of the money that visitors pay for the privilege of hunting there, wild animals become a resource to be protected. The local people get not only some of the cash but also the game meat. So "if it pays, it stays."

Trophy hunting helps curb poaching too. Game wardens and scouts, no matter how well trained or equipped, can't patrol everywhere at once. Hunters and their guides and trackers are out on the land paying attention to what's going on, and often they are the first to discover any signs of illegal killing of game.

Varmint Hunting

There's a third kind of hunting in America that is neither for the table nor for trophies. "Varmints" are pest species (vermin) such as woodchucks, prairie dogs, coyotes, and sometimes crows and starlings. These species are only minimally protected by game laws—generally there are no closed seasons or bag limits, or restrictions as to size or sex, but shooters must have hunting licenses and abide by basic sport-hunting conventions.

Varmints are wary and difficult to approach, and some are small targets. They are often shot at long range with ultra-accurate, small-bore rifles firing high-velocity ammunition and using specialized gear such as spotting scopes, shooting benches and rangefinders. Coyotes may be skinned for their fur, but rodents are usually left for scavengers and insects to clean up.

Varmints are shot for a variety of reasons, such as to curb property damage or to reduce the number of burrows that cattle or horses can potentially step in and break their legs. Coyotes often are targeted because it is felt that they hurt populations of game animals, such as deer and antelope. Birds like starlings, rock pigeons and Eurasian collared doves were introduced into the US and are considered invasive and not game animals, which is why there often are no seasons or bag limits.

Varmint hunting is generally regarded as much more environmentally friendly than killing destructive species with poison.

GAMEBIRDS

Shotguns are essential to hunt gamebirds, because birds are shot while they're on the wing. Hitting a strong, fast-flying bird while it's in the air is usually much harder than shooting a big animal with a rifle.

Upland gamebirds live on dry ground. "Uplands" are hillsides, meadows, woodlands and so on, any natural area that's drier than a marsh. In North America upland gamebirds include pheasants, a variety of grouse, chukar and Hungarian partridge, doves, woodcock, several kinds of quail and other similar species. Upland hunters walk the woods and fields with dogs trained to find birds, by scent, and then either flush them into the air for a shot or point them for the hunter to flush into the air. A wild bird rocketing out of its hiding place can be noisy and startling. Some gamebirds can hit 50 or 60 miles per hour. All have different flight patterns. A big pheasant flushing out of a cornfield and flying away in the open can be a fairly easy target; a ruffed grouse exploding from a hawthorn thicket and dodging away through thick pines is a very difficult target.

Huntable waterfowl includes ducks, geese, snipe, rails and sometimes cranes and swans. Waterfowlers often hide in blinds on the water or

Terry Allen

A West Texas cock pheasant. Bird hunting means walking the uplands with a keen-nosed dog, and then being able to hit a fast-flying target in the air.

in fields to wait for birds to approach close. They put out decoys to try to lure the birds out of the sky and use duck and goose calls to get their attention as they fly by.

It's possible to hunt gamebirds that have been specially raised and put out for the gun. The birds are bred in pens, but then they are released.

If they're released to fend for themselves when they're young, they behave and fly much more like wild birds than if they're let out close to when the hunters arrive.

❖

Bird Dogs

One of best things about hunting upland birds or waterfowl is having a dog to hunt with. Dogs are not only wonderful companions but also have a keen sense of smell, which helps the hunter find the game. A pointing dog (English setter, German shorthaired pointer, Brittany and others) sniffs out a gamebird's hiding place and then points to it by standing and staring at the spot until the hunter has caught up. Then the hunter moves in to flush the bird for a shot. Labradors, golden retrievers, cocker spaniels and other breeds are flushing dogs. They smell a hidden bird and then flush it for the hunter.

Dogs also find the shot birds. Because of their coloration, downed birds can be difficult to find without a dog's sharp nose. A dog can also track a wounded bird that's trying to get away.

A waterfowling dog sits by its hunter till it's time to fetch ducks and geese that fall in the water. Labrador and Chesapeake Bay retrievers and other dogs that don't mind cold water are bred especially for swimming out to a downed bird and bringing it back in their mouth.

❖

Flushing dogs, like this proud springer spaniel, not only flush the game, but they also retrieve dead birds and find wounded ones.

Terry Allen

TURKEYS

Wild turkeys look nothing like their white domestic counterparts. They are wild animals, camouflaged to suit their woodland habitat, and much stronger and warier than farm birds. At up to 25 pounds, the turkey is the largest of North America's gamebirds, and Benjamin Franklin thought that it, not the bald eagle, should be The Symbol of America. In the 1970s, state fish and game departments across the US set out to reestablish the turkey, which had disappeared from much of its original range. These programs succeeded beyond expectation, and now wild turkeys can be found again in about every state except Alaska.

Turkeys are the only birds that most hunters kill on the ground. In order not to destroy the meat, hunters try to shoot turkeys in the head. A turkey's head is a very small target, so the firearm of choice is a shotgun that delivers a tight cluster of shot big and heavy enough to be lethal out to 50 yards or so.

Turkeys are wary and have very sharp eyesight, so hunters camouflage themselves from head to toe. During the turkey's spring mating season, hunters sit in a likely spot and use a call that sounds like a female, or hen, to try to lure the male turkeys, the toms, into range.

National Wild Turkey Federation

Keen-eyed and wary, wild turkeys are a challenge for hunters, who have to lure them into range with calls and decoys. Benjamin Franklin thought the turkey, not the bald eagle, should be The Symbol of America.

HUNTING MANAGEMENT & ETHICS

Even in remote and sparsely populated corners of the world, hunting is strictly regulated by national or regional governments. Game laws are, or should be, based on wildlife science and are (or should be) designed to balance the annual "off-take" (how many animals of a certain species are killed) against the numbers needed to maintain healthy game populations. This is more difficult than it sounds because many factors, from forest fires to cli-

mate change, are involved, and they can vary from year to year.

Generally, these regulations establish hunting seasons (when hunting is allowed), zones and quotas, which may be a total for the area or how many of a particular animal an individual hunter is allowed to take per day or year. A hunting license often comes with a tag to attach to an animal, which sometimes has to be brought to a game-control station for examination. In some places and for some game these tags are awarded by lottery and can be very difficult to get.

License fees vary tremendously depending on whether a hunter is a resident or a nonresident of a particular state, a youngster or a senior citizen, and on the type of game and the region. For example, a junior small-game hunting license in New York State currently costs $5 per year, is valid for a number of animals and birds, and entitles the bearer to hunt freely within the laws of New York. At the other extreme, the trophy fee alone for an African rhino may be $100,000—on top of which the hunter must hire a safari company and pay its rates for camp, staff, vehicles and so on, and perhaps also a conservation fee to the local tribal commune.

Game departments or ministries also regulate the guns that hunters may use. Machine guns are illegal for hunting everywhere, and many countries ban semi-automatics also or limit how much ammunition they can hold. Hunting with handguns, blackpowder guns or bows is usually regulated separately. For safety, African countries usually forbid hunting dangerous game (such as lion and leopard, Cape buffalo, rhino and elephant) with cartridges below a certain power threshold.

Professional hunting guides are almost always government-certified and licensed. In many regions visiting hunters are required by law to hire a professional guide. In every state and some countries, particularly in Europe, hunters themselves, guided or not, have to pass qualification courses and tests before they're able to buy a hunting license—or even fire a gun. See "Hunter-Safety Courses" in "Getting Started."

The laws around guns and hunter education are intended to foster good sportsmanship and to improve the quality of the hunting experience, and especially to reduce accidents and promote safety. They have succeeded almost beyond expectation. Accidental shootings during hunting season inevitably draw attention, but statistically they are now almost non-existent.

Hunting isn't for everyone, but for people who accept that man is a natural predator and who have the desire to learn the skills, it can be both thrilling and deeply satisfying.

＋— ▇◆▇ —＋

Young Shooting Stars

Kids Don't Have to Look Far to Find Inspiring Role Models

Beyond the immediate enjoyment of a new interest, you may wonder what long-term benefit your youngster could ever realize from guns and shooting. Skill in stick-and-ball games, whether golf, baseball, tennis or lacrosse, can lead to college scholarships, sponsorships, travel, even professional careers and product endorsements. But what's out there for kids who are immersed in shooting targets instead of hoops?

As you'll see in the next chapter, there are interesting and respectable career options for people who want to work with guns. It's even possible (though difficult) to shoot for a living, and not just as a police or military marksman.

But that's far in the future. In the meantime, here are a few young shooters, grown up now, who made something of themselves (as our parents used to say). All it took was years of hard work, discipline and focus! You may be reassured, and your own offspring might even be impressed.

KIM RHODE, NATIONAL, WORLD & OLYMPIC CHAMPION

Kim Rhode (pronounced "Roadie") shoots 500 to 1,000 clay targets every practice day, sometimes seven days a week. That's hours of unbroken concentration despite recoil, noise and the effort of opening, closing and lifting an eight-plus-pound shotgun hundreds of times. It's also about $100 in clay pigeons per day and another $100 in cartridges fired through a shotgun that costs thousands. Stipends, sponsors, endorsements, coaching fees and personal appearances help offset these costs, but it takes years to get to such a level.

Kim Rhode, a US national trapshooting champion at the age of 13. Perazzi is the maker of her shotgun.

Kim grew up outside Los Angeles and attended public school. When some families went camping or to the beach, the Rhodes went shooting or hunting. When she turned 10, in 1989, Kim enrolled in the NRA Junior Shooting program and started to compete with a .22 rifle. Then, at her parents' gun club, she discovered the fun of flying targets and shotguns. Encouraged by her family and friends, Kim began to enter local competitions. At 13, she won her first national championship in doubles trap (shooting two clay targets launched at the same time, with a double-barreled gun). At 5 feet 4 inches, it was all she could do to swing a 12-gauge competition shotgun. At 17, in the 1996 Atlanta Olympics, Kim became the youngest female gold medalist in Olympic shooting history. She appeared on the Jay Leno show before the games; when she won, Leno sent her a dozen red roses.

The world-cup circuit takes competitors from the USA to Russia, Italy to Australia, China to Mexico, Egypt to Korea to the Dominican Republic and elsewhere as shooters jockey for trophies, medals, rankings and spots on their national teams. Kim was one of five women out of the 20 members of USA Shooting at the 2012 London Olympic Games. There she was the first woman to compete in both trap and skeet—and she became the first person ever, in any sport, to win a medal in five consecutive summer Olympics. Despite rain and wind and skies that went from blinding sun to dark overcast, Kim also set an Olympic skeet record, breaking 99 out of 100 targets. She had prepared for English weather by training in Oregon and northern California.

In her 30s and married, Kim is no longer a "young phenom," but that's exactly what she was. Family and friends recognized her talent and nurtured it—her father, a professional deep-sea diver, is still her coach—and her own determination and skills took her to the top.

Kim has a champion's hand-eye coordination and muscle memory, but her training "se-

Kim Rhode at 17, in the 1996 Atlanta games, became the youngest female gold medalist in Olympic shooting history. At the 2012 London games she was the first woman to compete in both trap and skeet—and became the first person ever, in any sport, to win a medal in five consecutive summer Olympics.

cret," she said, is her love of video games. The Rhode family also has its own way of dealing with pressure. In London her father said, "We never shot to win. Never. She didn't come here to win. She came here to have a good time. It's just like we told her when she was a kid: It's just the cherry on top of the cake if you win. '*Hey, good job, let's go down to get an ice cream cone.*'

"There's no pressure. You're competing against yourself. If you lose, your husband's going to love you just as much; your parents are going to love you just as much. So go out there and have a good time."

Off the field, Kim collects first editions of children's books and restores classic cars. She spent five years building a replica Cobra 427 roadster. She studied veterinary medicine and has designed a line of women's shooting attire. There's even an iPhone app called "Kim Rhode's Outdoor Shooting," available for $2.99 from iTunes.

MATT EMMONS, US NATIONAL SHOOTING TEAM

*I*f Kim Rhode owes her success to family, determination, dogged persistence and skill with a shotgun, Olympic medalist Matt Emmons' story seems to revolve around adversity, luck both good and bad, sportsmanship—*and* mental precision and skill with a rifle.

Matt grew up in New Jersey and began to shoot competitively in high school after a friend, an FBI firearms instructor, suggested he give it a try. (As a star baseball player, Matt once pitched a no-hitter.) In 1997, when he was 17, Matt won the 50-meter prone and three-position (120 shots over three hours—kneeling, standing and prone) events in the US national championships. This led to a spot on the University of Alaska's Nanooks rifle team, where he won three individual and four team titles in National Collegiate Athletic Association competition. Then it was on to the International Shooting Sport Federation World Cup, the USA Shooting team and Olympic competition.

It's a tossup whether the travel or practice is more grueling. To consistently drop his .22 bullets into a dime-size circle half a football field distant, Matt shoots for four to six hours daily—on top of two hours in the gym every day. He managed to earn a degree in Management & Finance too.

Matt Emmons may be the best rifle shot in the world, but then there are his trademark brushes with fickle fortune. Before the 2004 Olympics in Athens, his rifle was sabotaged. Someone—a jealous competitor?—damaged its precisely machined bore, apparently with a screwdriver. He borrowed a teammate's rifle and

Matt Emmons, Olympic champion and USA Shooting heart-throb, after the 2004 Athens games. This is the rifle he had to borrow from a teammate.

won not only the Olympic trials, but then also the 50-meter gold medal with it. (Imagine winning a marathon in shoes custom-fitted to someone else.) "A year later [the teammate] retired and I got to keep the gun I won the Olympics with," Emmons said, "and I've competed up until now with that same gun."

There's more. With one gold medal in the bag in Athens, Matt was leading in the 50-meter three-position with one shot to go. It was almost impossible for an athlete of Emmons' skill to lose from this position, but he did. A bit too relaxed, Matt put his final bullet into the target next to his, the one belonging to an Austrian competitor. His total score fell from first place to last. A Chinese shooter collected the win.

That evening, with the shooting done, Emmons joined friends at a beer garden to try to forget his blunder. A Czech shooter named Katerina Kurkova introduced herself and told Matt how sorry she was about what happened and how she admired his handling of the situation.

Long afterward, Emmons said, "At that time I just knew who she was; we'd never spoken. But we hit it off really well, we started dating a year later, and we were married in 2007. She's now Katerina Emmons." In 2009 the Emmons had a daughter and named her Julie.

In the summer of 2010 Matt was diagnosed with thyroid cancer. After surgery and weeks of therapy, he was pronounced cancer-free and returned to training.

Matt and Katy Emmons continued to shoot for their national teams. In 2008, at the Beijing Olympics, Katerina won gold for the Czech Republic. Matt earned a silver in the 50-meter prone. Then, in the three-position round, Matt again held a solid lead—and stroked his trigger prematurely, blew the last shot and dropped to fourth place. Again the gold went to a Chinese shooter. After a moment of heartbreak, Matt did the only thing he could do: He began to laugh, ruefully, and turned to find Katy in the audience. "Your life is not defined by one shot or by one competition," he later told NBC News.

One more time: On the final day of shooting at the London Olympics of 2012, Matt faced his nemesis again, the 50-meter three-position event. And again he unaccountably misfired his last shot. But this time he dropped only to third. A reporter concluded that Emmons "can be content with the real bronze, the gold for candor and—what the heck—let's give him another gold for heartbreak."

THE CALIFORNIA GRIZZLIES

Wayne Christensen

Members of the 2012 California Grizzles and Cubs junior rifle teams. The groups, ages 13 to 20, train and compete at local ranges, and Grizzlies are eligible to compete in the National Matches at Camp Perry, Ohio, each August. The Cubs shoot .22 rimfire rifles before they move up to Grizzly status and .223 centerfire rifles for longer-range competition.

The Grizzlies were formed in 2003 to teach firearms safety and marksmanship as well as leadership and citizenship. With the help of adult instructors, the Grizzlies mentor Cubs and younger shooters on other teams. The teams are affiliated with the NRA, the California Rifle and Pistol Association and the Civilian Marksmanship Program.

Careers That Involve Guns

The Business of the Shooting Sports

If your youngster's interest in guns or shooting surpasses all else, don't despair. There are many professions (besides the police and military) that involve shooting or working with guns. The National Shooting Sports Foundation, a trade association with more than 7,000 members, calculates that nearly 600,000 people are employed in the shooting sports in the US today, by manufacturers, distributors and retailers of guns, ammunition and related products and services, shooting ranges, sportsmen's organizations, media and sales companies and so on. Most of the work carried out by these people, be they business executives, account reps, financial analysts, shipping clerks, journalists or copywriters, is the same as what needs to be done in the amalgamated widget industry, with one significant difference: Many of these individuals are shooters. They've figured out a way to make a living from their passions. Is there a better way to spend one's working years?

The core of the shooting-sports trade is gunmaking, and the oldest documented manufacturing company in business anywhere today is a gunmaker. Beretta, based in northern Italy, has a receipt dated October 3, 1526, for 185 musket barrels sold to the city-state of Venice. Today Beretta has factories around the world and is one of the largest and most successful suppliers of sporting, police and military firearms.

In addition to Pietro Beretta, men named Whitney, Lefaucheux, Forsyth, Colt, Winchester, Remington, Gatling, Maxim, Mauser, Lee, Lebel, Whitworth, Mannlicher, Rigby, Browning, Thompson, Kalashnikov, Garand and many more—designers or makers of guns—played crucial roles in history. Cities in Britain, France, Germany, Austria, Belgium, Italy, Russia, Spain and the United States became centers of gun manufacturing. School systems and professional associations were created to support gunmaking.

Below is a list of some professions that are truly hands-on with guns. Some of them require the latest in computer technology; one has hardly changed in 500 years. The information is also in *The Gun Book for Boys*, in different form, so your youngster can "discover" it all by himself or herself.

―――※♦≡―――

GUNMAKER

A gunmaker builds firearms in mass quantities or one at a time or something in between. Small or large, gunmakers often focus on certain markets: They build a particular type of handgun, or they concentrate on military or police needs, big-game hunting, competitive shotgun shooting and so on. A few build replicas of historic old guns.

Mass-production gunmaking is simply manufacturing. There are tools and methods to learn, from design to fabrication (i.e., operating machinery) and from assembly and quality control to promotion, sales, distribution, accounting and management. Smaller or less-automated makers employ specialists: craftsmen who carve and checker gunstocks, machinists who bore and rifle barrels, actioners who make the lockwork, finishers who assemble the pieces and test them. These are skilled people who often learned their trades in technical school or as apprentices.

Anyone interested in designing guns—which must be safe, reliable, accurate and often commercially practical—should be trained in mechanical engineering.

When it comes to custom-built guns, which require much hand craftsmanship and may carry six-figure price tags, the best of these workers are often self-employed; they set up workshops at home and operate as freelancers, known in Europe as "outworkers to the trade." There are few outworkers in the US because there are just a handful of such gunmakers here. American gun companies are almost exclusively involved in mass production.

FORENSIC SCIENTIST

Crime labs have been supporting the criminal justice system in the US since the 1920s, but it wasn't until *CSI* started on TV that the public got interested in them. Officially known as criminalistics or forensic laboratories, they are staffed with specialists such as document and fingerprint examiners, toxicologists, crime-scene and laboratory technicians, photographers and firearms examiners.

Technicians generally gather evidence (strands of hair or fibers, shards of glass, bullets, blood, fingerprints, ashes, tissue and bone, weapons and so on) at crime scenes. Back at the lab, scientists analyze these materials to try to unravel exactly how a crime happened.

Forensic firearms examiners study evidence with optical and electronic instruments, and then interpret their findings. Sometimes they testify in court. Often they test-fire guns, and then compare bullets and cartridge cases with suspect firearms. They work with police, prosecutors, defense attorneys and other experts who may be examining the same guns for DNA evidence or fingerprints.

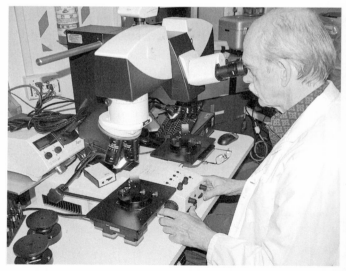

Torrey Johnson using a comparison microscope at a California Dept. of Justice forensics lab. Firearms examiners often test-fire guns, and then compare bullets and cartridge cases with suspect firearms to see if they can be tied to a crime.

There are about 400 crime labs serving law-enforcement agencies in the US. A Bachelor of Science degree in biology or chemistry is usually the minimum requirement for getting a job in one of them. It's an interesting and rewarding career for someone who likes firearms and science.

PROFESSIONAL HUNTER

Peter Hathaway Capstick wrote the following in a 1984 book called *Safari, the Last Adventure*:

Professional Hunter Wanted:

Young active man interested in low and infrequent pay to play bwana in remote bushveld. Must be proven raconteur and socialite without liver trouble, expert card player, bartender, caterer, barbecuer, philosopher, African historian. Experience in sanitary engineering, local architecture, labor relations, navigation, medicine and pharmacology, botany, zoology, ichthyology, mineralogy, entomology, butchery, taxidermy, dietetics, optics, photography and radio operation essential. Applicant should speak at least two black African languages fluently as well as English and one other modern European tongue. A solid knowledge of mechanics, driving, gunsmithing, toxicology, ballistics, tracking, marksmanship, hand loading and experience as a professional bodyguard are required.

Benefits are: Twenty-four-hour day, unlimited fresh air, including rain, sun and dust, no medical, dental or life insurance and no retirement benefits. Applicant should supply his own rifles. Vehicles on a per diem basis.

Capstick meant this to contrast with the Hollywood impression of a White Hunter as some sort of minor god who looked like Burt Lancaster and could sweep both beautiful women and charging elephants off their feet with equal ease. The reality, as Capstick knew very well, is much less glamorous.

Professional Hunter Jofie Lamprecht, right, with a happy client in Africa. The hours are long, the conditions can be awful and the pay isn't great, but for a certain kind of person, there's no other life.

Non-hunters are often surprised to learn that safari hunting is not only still possible but also more popular than ever. In all African countries where sport hunting is allowed, it is heavily regulated for safety and conservation, and it earns substantial fees for wildlife departments and local villages. The guides are no longer called White Hunters, however, and many safari professionals these days are, in fact, black. They're now called PHs, Professional Hunters, and they have to take certification courses and pass examinations to earn the title. Generally, there are plains-game and dangerous-game PH licenses. Taking clients after dangerous game, such as lion, elephant, rhino, Cape buffalo and leopard, is more risky than stalking antelope, and it calls for a higher standard of skill and experience.

Anyone can become an African PH, given enough determination and effort. The work, however, only gets harder after passing the test and joining a safari company. The hours are long, the conditions can be awful, and the clients can

be inept (or worse). But for a certain kind of person, there's no other life.

In the US, regulations governing professional hunting guides differ from state to state. The best way to research this is by clicking around on a government Website for "becoming a hunting guide." Whether in Montana or in Namibia, guides almost always start out as trainees or apprentices in established companies.

GAME WARDEN

Game wardens are police officers who monitor hunters and fishermen (and sometimes boaters, snowmobilers, hikers, back-country skiers and others who participate in outdoor recreation). Wardens spend much of their time in the field checking fishing and hunting licenses and enforcing the laws about bag limits and what sorts of game and guns and hunting or fishing methods are legal in their district.

Wardens graduate from police-academy-style training programs. They are uniformed and armed and are issued vehicles—pickup trucks, boats, snowmobiles, even light planes and helicopters. They may use the Internet and forensic investigation techniques to break up gangs of wildlife smugglers or go out on snowshoes with dogs to find lost hunters or hikers. If dangerous animals have to be dealt with—a sheep-killing bear, for example, or a mountain lion that attacked a hiker—game wardens are called in.

State game wardens combine the crime-fighting skills of police officers with the woodsmanship of hunters and fishermen.

Some states employ professional hunters to track down such problem animals.

PROFESSIONAL SHOOTER

This means becoming an exceptional shot, which requires a certain natural talent and the willingness and opportunity to practice for hours each week, if not daily. And

then there's the matter of finding employment.

Companies sometimes hire experts to help sell their guns by demonstrating them at fairs and other public events or at private demos for

Steve and Aaron Gould, known as GBX, for Gould Brothers Exhibition Team, are part of the Winchester Repeating Arms pro staff. They travel around the US to stage exhibition shooting shows.

military or police buyers. Certain world-class competition shooters may get a paycheck from a gunmaker. Members of national Olympic shoot-

ing teams may have their living expenses paid by sponsors so that they can practice and compete without the distraction of a job.

The teaching pro or the club champion at a sporting-clays course might get a gun each season and have his or her ammunition provided. A well-known hunting guide might get guns and ammunition and maybe even a truck, if he's featured in a TV series. But this isn't earning a living; the pro and the guide still have to attract paying clients.

The odds of becoming a full-time professional shooter are probably worse than landing a spot in the NFL or NBA—which pays a lot better.

GUNSHOP EMPLOYEE/OWNER

Many a gunshop owner or gun-department employee at a sporting-goods megastore was once a kid fascinated with guns. However, the day-to-day work of retail sales or owning a small business can easily overwhelm the enjoyable aspects of being in the gun trade. Many gunshop owners say, regretfully, that they used to do a lot of shooting until they got into the shooting business.

Managing cash flow, tax records and employees can be a job unto itself. So is figuring out how to bring in more customers, and then having the right mix of guns, ammunition and other products on hand for them. In addition, firearms retailers have to

Retail businesses such as specialty gunshops and sporting-goods stores employ many people who grew up interested in guns and shooting.

be specially licensed, and gun and sometimes ammunition sales are controlled and have to be recorded and reported.

A young person who knows guns is a good candidate to be a sales clerk in a gunshop. If it works out, the owner may be thrilled to find an employee to whom he can sell the business when it's time to retire.

SHOOTING WRITER

Worldwide, there are hundreds of media—in print, on TV and on the Web—that deliver information to shooters about guns, ammunition and gear, shooting techniques, destinations, people, collectible or historic firearms and so on. Many books are published on these subjects too. This kind of writing can be an interesting, though rarely well-paid, career.

Shooting writers may travel widely, get samples of guns and gear, be invited to visit gunmakers or go on hunts, and meet famous people. Some gun writers become famous themselves in a small way.

Just as in almost every other firearms-related career, simply knowing a lot about guns isn't enough. To write successfully about guns (or hunting or firearms history or whatever) means becoming a good writer too. As the saying goes, if you want to write an article or a book, you have to read one first. Writers read—a lot.

Young writers join the school newspaper or Website. A few eventually get in touch with the editors of magazines and offer ideas for stories. Editors need writers, and publications are always looking for fresh talent.

GUNSMITH

A gunsmith (as opposed to a gunmaker) repairs or modifies guns. Some gunsmiths are generalists who mount a scope on a customer's rifle one day, and the next day fix a broken part or do a strip-and-clean. Others specialize in, for example, fine-tuning competition pistols or big-game rifles or restoring old guns. Some gunsmiths now even have cable-TV shows.

Many gunsmiths are self-employed, and some also buy and sell guns. Today anyone who wants to work on firearms is well advised to go to a vocational school to learn about metallurgy, welding, woodworking, finishing and so on. On top of the various tax burdens of self-employment, buying and selling guns and gun parts requires federal licensing and records-keeping.

Gunsmith Dale Tate of California opens up the chokes in a pair of shotgun barrels with a honing tool. A gunmaker builds guns; a gunsmith repairs or modifies them.

ARMORER

Large police departments and every branch of the military have armorers, gunsmiths who maintain their members' weapons. Armorers often also customize guns, ammunition and gear for special uses (sniping, arctic or desert warfare, match competition and so on). Armorers often work with manufacturers on improvements to guns, ammunition, sights and even holsters, carrying slings and features like suppressors (silencers).

Specialists who build and take care of the guns used in movies and on TV are armorers also. Many of those guns are real but have been modified in some way for safety or special effects. Movie machine guns, for example, are often converted to operate on natural gas, so they don't have to fire live ammunition. This kind of work takes not only professional gunsmithing skills but also engineering know-how as well as imagination.

ENGRAVER

More and more of the engraving that decorates guns is applied with an automated laser or by acid-etching. The best guns, however, will always be engraved by hand. Engraving, or "drawing on steel," requires a steady hand, an artist's eye and a knowledge of metals. The tools are simple: an assortment of chisels, gravers and scribers; a special vise to hold the gun; a good chair and lighting; and some sort of magnifying lens. Some engravers also use an electric cutter like a dentist's drill.

Engraver Lisa Tomlin at work in her studio in Virginia.

It's possible to go to school to become an engraver, but many engravers learn by themselves or as apprentices to established masters. All engravers, whether self-taught or schooled, have the natural ability to draw.

Some engravers start out working for studios, decorating not just guns but also knives, money clips and so on. If they love the work and have a talent for it, they may go out on their own as independent craftsmen. (Many engravers are women, by the way.) The best engravers often have several years' worth of commissions lined up. Their work doesn't make guns shoot any better, but it adds beauty and many thousands of dollars of value.

GUNSMITHING SCHOOLS

There are many online, video and correspondence gunsmithing programs as well as those programs offered by these schools. Contact the American Custom Gunmakers Guild (www.acgg.org) for more information about educational opportunities.

American Gunsmithing Institute (www.americangunsmith.com): more than 200 video courses.

Ashworth College (www.ashworthcollege.edu), Norcross, GA: online and correspondence courses.

Brownells-Trinidad American Firearms Technology Institute (www.trinidadstate.edu/gunsmithing), Trinidad, CO: an advanced program designed to teach gunsmithing-shop operations and management.

Colorado School of Trades (www.schooloftrades.edu), Lakewood, CO: accredited gunsmithing school as part of the largest gunsmithing repair facility in the US.

NRA Short-Term Gunsmithing Schools (www.nragunsmithing.com): courses from several days to two weeks with housing available at some campuses at Murray State College, Tishomingo, OK; Lassen Community College, Susanville, CA; Trinidad State Junior College, Trinidad, CO; Montgomery Community College, Troy, NC.

Penn Foster Career School (www.pennfoster.edu), Scranton, PA: online and distance learning courses.

Pennsylvania Gunsmith School (www.pagunsmith.edu), Pittsburgh: two-year (16 months) accredited program as a member of the Accrediting Commission of Career Schools and Colleges of Technology.

Piedmont Technical College (www.ptc.edu), South Carolina: accredited courses in gunsmithing and advanced gunsmithing.

Pine Technical College (www.pinetech.edu), Pine City, MN: accredited courses in all phases of gun repair and gunsmithing.

Trinidad State Junior College (www.trinidadstate.edu/gunsmithing), Trinidad, CO: TSJC began offering gunsmithing courses in 1947. This developed into a two-year Gunsmithing Degree Program, with courses at basic and advanced levels that offer concepts and skills needed by a professional gunsmith.

Yavapai College Gunsmithing School (www.yc.edu), Prescott, AZ: Associate of Applied Science Degree in Gunsmithing as well as a gunsmithing certificate.

Engraving Schools: Contact the Firearms Engravers Guild of America (www.fega.com) for information on educational opportunities.

GRS Training Center (www.grstrainingcenter.com), Emporia, KS: basic, intermediate and advanced gun-engraving courses in four-day sessions.

Mike Dubber Engraving Studio (www.firearmsengraving.com), Evansville, IN: studio instruction in basic, intermediate and advanced gun engraving lasting three to five days.

John Weyerts School of Engraving (www.engravinginstruction.com), Alpine, TX: studio instruction in basic, intermediate and advanced gun engraving lasting five days.

Montgomery Community College (www.montgomery.edu), Montgomery, NC: basic Metal Engraving Certificate and Metal Engraving diploma programs.

Youth Programs in the Shooting Sports

Help Is Available—Lots of Help

If you log onto the Internet and type "youth shooting programs" into your search engine, you'll be astonished by the variety and sheer volume of what's out there. (Shooters are serious about bringing new people into their sport and about teaching safe gun-handling.)

Here is a brief overview of the major organizations that create or support these programs and a sampling of relevant Web addresses. (Also refer to "Getting Started.")

NRA

The NRA was founded in 1871 by Col. William C. Church and Gen. George Wingate to promote and encourage rifle marksmanship among civilians. It is now the oldest civil-rights group in the US and America's top advocate for gun ownership as well as firearms safety. The NRA offers or sanctions training courses for everyone from beginning shooters to shooting instructors and police officers.

In 1903 the NRA established rifle clubs at many universities, colleges and military academies. Today the NRA offers youth programs and camps that teach firearms safety as well as wildlife art, journalism, leadership and team building. More than a million young people participate in NRA-sanctioned shooting-sports programs with other groups such as the Boy Scouts of America, the American Legion and the Jaycees. The NRA Youth Hunter Education Challenge has to date helped more than 40,000 young hunters (in 43

states and three Canadian provinces) build on the skills learned in basic hunter-education programs.

The NRA has 4.3 million members and is affiliated with similar organizations in other countries. Many prominent Americans have been members of the NRA, including Presidents Ulysses S. Grant (who also served as president of the NRA), Theodore Roosevelt, John F. Kennedy, Ronald Reagan and George H.W. Bush.

The NRA is based in Fairfax, Virginia. It publishes a number of influential magazines and has a vast Website at www.nra.org.

• NRA shooting programs for young people can be accessed at www.nrahq.org/youth/.

• See also www.nrahq.org/youth/organization. asp.

SCOUTING

Scouting is a century-old world-wide movement that fosters the physical, mental and spiritual development of boys and girls. Combining formal education with the experiences of practical outdoor activities became the cornerstone of Scouting culture, along with distinctive ranks and uniforms, camp patches and merit badges that denote achievement. By 2011 Scouting had more than 41 million members throughout the world. The slogan "Be Prepared" is recognized everywhere as Scouting's motto.

Scouting started when Lt. Gen. Robert Baden-Powell held the first encampment for boys in England in 1907. In 1908 his illustrated book, *Scouting for Boys: A Handbook for Instruction in Good Citizenship*, set forth the principles of scouting as he saw them and as influenced by his military background. Scouting for boys grew into three major divisions based on age: Cub Scouts, Boy Scouts and Rover Scouts. In 1910 the Girl Guides were formed with similar age groups: Brownie Guide, Girl Guide and Girl Scout, and Ranger Guide.

The most popular Scouting organizations in America include the Cub Scouts of America, Boy Scouts of America, Explorer Scouts of America, Brownies, Girl Scouts of America and Camp Fire USA. All have informative Websites.

Many people earned the Marksmanship merit badge on the rifle range at Scout camp. That was replaced recently by merit badges in Rifle Shooting and Shotgun Shooting. Scouting has also partnered with the NSSF (below) to develop national shooting programs for kids, start-

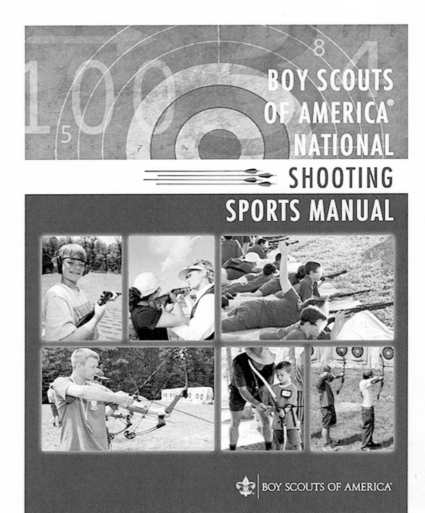

ing with a BB gun curriculum in the Cub Scout Academics & Sports Program and continuing into rifle and shotgun shooting in Boy Scouts and Venturing Scouts.

• www.scouting.org/scoutsource/Healthand Safety/GSS/gss07.aspx.

• A downloadable copy of the *BSA National Shooting Sports Manual* is at scouting.org/filestore/Outdoor%20Program/pdf/30931_WB.pdf.

NATIONAL SHOOTING SPORTS FOUNDATION

The NSSF was established in 1961 and has more than 7,000 members. As the trade organization for the American firearms, ammunition, hunting and shooting-sports industry, NSSF has considerable clout. Members include manufacturers, distributors and retailers of guns, ammunition and related products and services as well as shooting ranges, sportsmen's organizations and media firms and individuals. The NSSF offers programs, Websites, publications, events and services that promote and preserve responsible business practices, gun ownership and safety, and opportunities in the shooting sports.

Through programs such as Families Afield, Project ChildSafe and the Scholastic Clay Target Program (now administered by the Scholastic Shooting Sports Foundation), NSSF has reached thousands of young people. The First Shots program continues to help shooting ranges all over America introduce newcomers (youth and adults) to the shooting sports.

The NSSF is headquartered in Newtown, Connecticut. It owns and sponsors the annual SHOT (Shooting, Hunting, Outdoor Trade) Show, which attracts more than 60,000 professional exhibitors and attendees from around the world, and its Website, at www.nssf.org, covers everything from industry news to job openings.

The NSSF and NRA often work together to sponsor or promote shooting-related legislation such as the recent bipartisan Target Practice and Marksmanship Training Support Act, intended to "ensure that shooters and hunters have high-quality public facilities at which to participate in recreational shooting sports and to learn about firearms safety."

• The NSSF offers a downloadable *Parent's Guide to Recreational Shooting for Youngsters* at www.nssf.org/lit/ParentsGuide10.pdf.

A PARENT'S GUIDE TO RECREATIONAL SHOOTING FOR YOUNGSTERS

WWW.NSSF.ORG

The NSSF has linked a comprehensive directory of shooting ranges across the US to a smartphone app called Where2Shoot. It's available for free (ages 17 and up) from the Sports category in the iTunes store.

• See also www.nssf.org/shooting/learn/.

• NSSF's First Shots introductory program has a state directory: www.nssf.org/FirstShots.

4-H

Launched in Ohio by A.B. Graham in 1902, 4-H has grown into a global organization—there are 4-H clubs in 80 countries—and is the largest youth-development organization in America, fostering a hands-on approach to leadership and innovation. There are now more than 6.5 million boys and girls participating in programs focused on science, health and citizenship in 90,000 clubs, and more than 60 million Americans are 4-H alumni. The four Hs stand for Head (for managing and thinking), Heart (relating, caring) Hands (giving, working) and Health (being, living). Many people think that 4-H is a rural organization for farm kids, but it has clubs in the inner city and the suburbs as well, and affiliations with many state universities. 4-H has an excellent shooting-sports curriculum that teaches "Skills for Life—Activity for a Lifetime": www.4-hshootingsports.org/site_map.php.

OTHER PROGRAMS

One of the largest gun companies in the US is **Daisy**, the venerable maker of BB and pellet guns. Many shooters start with a Daisy, a fact that the company has capitalized on by creating its own array of shooting curricula, safety rules, books and competitions. For more information, visit www.daisy.com/education.html.

The Scholastic Clay Target Program (www.shootsctp.org) is an "educational-athletic organization that exists to introduce school-age youths to the clay target sports and to facilitate their continued involvement by providing, promoting, and perpetuating opportunities to safely and enjoyably participate and compete in a high-quality, team-based sport led by trained adult coaches focused on enhancing the personal growth and development of their athletes."

Various **regional shooting clubs** offer SCTP-affiliated programs such as this: http://mytbsc.com/summer-campsfall-youth-scholastic-shooting-program.

USA Shooting (www.usashooting.org), the governing body of the United States Olympic Team, which competes in rifle, pistol and shotgun events, has a Junior Olympic Shooting Program.

The **American Legion** has a Junior Shooting Sports Program. For more information, visit www.legion.org/shooting.

The US government teaches shooting through its **Civilian Marksmanship Program** (www.odcmp.org), chartered in 1903.

The **Youth Shooting Sports Alliance** (www.youthshootingsa.com) has an online directory of youth shooting programs organized by state and

by type of shooting: shotgun, rifle, handgun, air rifles/BB guns, muzzleloaders and archery.

Junior Shooters Magazine (www.juniorshooters. net) publishes three print issues per year and posts articles on its Website weekly.

+—+ ≈◊≋ +—+

CONSERVATION & HUNTING ORGANIZATIONS

Many national conservation and outdoor associations have created young-hunter programs that often include instruction in shooting as well as firearms handling and safety. Ducks Unlimited and Pheasants Forever/Quail Forever may be the largest of these groups; others include Safari Club International, Dallas Safari Club, Quail Unlimited, the Ruffed Grouse Society, the National Wild Turkey Federation, the Rocky Mountain Elk Foundation, Whitetails Unlimited, the Mule Deer Foundation and more. Each has regional and state chapters. Visit their individual Websites to look for activities for youngsters.

+—+ ≈◊≋ +—+

Acknowledgements

Joe Coogan, Rich Eastman, Naomi Farmer, Jim Gleason, William King, Jim Koudela, Ed Land, Glenn Sapir, Don Stackhouse and Ralph Stuart helped us with this book. Thanks also go to our patient wives—Sue, Marilyn and Kathy. And we are especially grateful to Karim and Hayden Baker and to Lisa and Chris Mayers, mothers and sons who "proof-tested" the manuscript of this book and *The Gun Book for Boys* and whose enthusiasm and comments were so helpful.

Silvio Calabi
Steve Helsley
Roger Sanger

INDEX

The Authors

Silvio Calabi was a magazine editor and publisher for 30 years. He is a Knight of the International Order of St. Hubertus and a member of Safari Club International and the Namibian Professional Hunting Association. With Roger Sanger, he co-founded the Gold Medal Concours d'Elegance of Fine Guns. With Sanger and Helsley, he wrote *Hemingway's Guns* and *Rigby: A Grand Tradition*. He lives on the coast of Maine.

Steve Helsley, of El Dorado Hills, California, is a retired law-enforcement executive, a consultant to the National Rifle Association and a technical adviser to the Association of Firearm and Tool Mark Examiners. He is also a firearms historian and photographer and a widely published authority on vintage and tactical guns. He has collaborated with Sanger and Calabi on other books and many articles for shooting magazines.

Roger G. Sanger founded the California Side By Side Society and served as its president for many years. In 2001, with Calabi, he co-founded the Gold Medal Concours d'Elegance of Fine Guns and then, with Helsley, the Western Side By Side Championships. Sanger is a Knight of the International Order of St. Hubertus and has written for *Shooting Sportsman* Magazine. He lives in Carmel, California, and Sun Valley, Idaho.